FOUNDATIONS OF THE FAITH

D0503368

MORAN ROSENBLIT AND BARUCH KORMAN

By: Moran Rosenblit and Baruch Korman

All Rights Reserved © July 2017

ISBN 978-164-008-337-0

All Scriptural citations are translated from the original Hebrew, Aramaic, and Greek in a most literal manner.

We stress the importance of the personal reading of Scripture, beginning in Genesis and continuing through Revelation.

Please visit us at hope4israel.org and loveisrael.org to learn more.

Printed in the United States, July 2017

הודפס בארה''ב, תמח תשע"ז

CONTENTS

FUNDAMENTAL PRINCIPLES

Most people in the world wonder what the true meaning of their lives is, and thus they ask philosophical questions about life. For example: Is there life after death? Why do bad things happen? Does anything exist other than the world we live in? The Bible describes the Source of Life in the world in general and the Source of Life of Man in particular. One of the principles discovered through the Bible is that it is impossible to understand life completely, without recognizing the Creator of the Universe and the Giver of Life. Understanding the description of the Creation of the Universe by the hand of the Holy One is a very important matter, therefore it is important to pay attention to the description immediately before Creation:

> **The Earth was chaos and void, and darkness was over the abyss. (Genesis 1:2)**

We know that God is omnipotent. The fact that He created the world, as it is written, "the Earth was chaos and void," indicates a more meaningful point. The proper interpretation of the expression chaos and void "תהו ובהו" (*tohu va-vohu*) is "disorder." That is, when the Holy One created the Earth, it was not in the proper state at first. In other words, the Earth was in need of repair. During the six days of the creation of the universe, the Creation went through the first repair, as it is written: **"God saw all which He did and behold (it was) very good; and it was evening and it was morning, the sixth day"** (Genesis 1:31).

In the book of Genesis, the story of the sin of the Tree of Knowledge is told, the tree from which Adam and Eve ate, despite the fact that God forbade them to do so. Once again, after this sin, the world was in need of repair. This is due to the separation that was made between God and mankind, a matter that constitutes both the reason that we do not experience happiness, contentment, peace, and satisfaction more fully and the reason that God desires to be our portion. Our lives lack the divine order, and to fix this situation, we must understand the conception of God properly. It is not by chance that it is written at the end of the verse quoted above that **"darkness was over the abyss."** The meaning of the word "darkness" is a lack of understanding; not just a lack of understanding in general, but rather a lack of understanding God's will and His plans. The aforementioned verse ends with the words, **"And the Spirit of God is hovering over the waters,"** meaning that the Spirit of the LORD was between the earth and the heavens.

Through the Spirit of God, mankind can receive a spiritual understanding about the Holy One's will, plans, and other questions about the meaning of life. In the next verse it is written:

> And God said, "Let there be light," and there was light. (Genesis 1:3)

From here we learn that the only solution to the darkness is the light of the LORD. The Torah is not speaking of any ordinary light, rather about Divine Revelation (the Word of God), and this is the reason that the verse opens with the words, **"And God said."** From these words we understand that it is impossible to understand the true meaning of life without understanding the Word of God. How do we know that the light spoken of in the verse above is not just any ordinary light? Because God did not create the lights in the firmament of heaven until the fourth day of creation (Genesis 1:14). The Word of God is likened to light many times in Scripture, for example:

> A lamp to my feet is Your word and a light to my path. (Psalms 119:105)

Therefore, if one wishes to find the true meaning of life, he requires the enlightenment that can be found only in the Word of God. From the next verse we learn why the Scriptures (the Word of God) are so important to understanding the will of the Holy One:

> God saw the light that (it is) good, and God separated between the light and the darkness. (Genesis 1:4)

Only through the Word of God is it possible to separate between light and darkness (between good and evil). Why? Because God presents the reader with the Divine Truth. When the earth is in its primal form, darkness abounds, and until the Holy One spoke, there was no light in the world. In the same way, after the sin of the Tree of Knowledge, mankind was also in a state of darkness, and accordingly was in need of the Truth (light) of God in order to emerge from the darkness. The Torah says that the LORD created the light in one day: **"And God called the light Day and the darkness He called Night, and it was evening and it was morning, day One."**

It is interesting to see that the Torah used a different expression for the rest of the days of creation from that of first day (literally: **day one**), the rest of the days of the week are called the second day, third day, fourth day, fifth day, sixth day, and the seventh day. Why does the Torah call this day "יום אחד" (*yom echad*) **"one day,"** or instead of the "first day"? For this name is meant to emphasize the idea of "unity." The LORD wants to have a relationship with humanity, and like all relationships, it must be based on truth (Divine Truth). Without a proper and honest relationship between the Holy One and us, we will not be able to understand the true meaning of our lives.

───── **The Meaning of the Sabbath and Understanding of Priorities** ─────

In Hebrew, there is an expression that many are familiar with from the Sabbath song Lechah Dodi, "Last in deed, first in thought." According to this, it was no coincidence that God created man on the sixth day as the last creation. For man is the purpose of creation. What is the meaning of the close proximity between the creation of man and the seventh day? The answer is that the Sabbath was sanctified by God especially to strengthen the relationship between God and humanity. The fact that mankind was the last thing that the LORD created before the Sabbath shows how important humanity is to God. In addition, from here we learn that the Sabbath is not a reward or payment for hard work all week long, but rather it is an essential matter for every person. To be able to fully and positively appreciate the six other days of the week, we must understand the true meaning of the Sabbath and all of the positive benefits of this holy day. God sanctified the Sabbath to produce order in our lives, and only through true connection between God and ourselves will we be able to receive the necessary inspiration to know His will and abide by his commands. This is the process that we grow and develop all throughout our lives. There are those who ask, "Why the Sabbath day in particular? Is God busy on the rest of the days and only available to us on the Sabbath?" Most certainly not, yet we cannot avoid the fact that God blessed the seventh day in a special way:

> **And were finished the heavens and the earth, and all the host (Armies) of them. And God completed on the seventh day His work which He did, and He rested on the seventh day from all His work which He did. And God blessed the seventh day and He made it holy, because on it He rested from all His work which God created to do. (Genesis 2:1–3)**

According to this verse, what was the first thing that God did after creating mankind?

The answer is that He stopped or rested. We can say with certainty that the LORD did not rest because He was tired, rather that He wanted to spend time with man. The fact that God blessed and sanctified the seventh day, and indeed the seventh day was the first thing that the first man experienced, reveals to the reader that out of everything that was created, humanity is the first priority of the Holy One, blessed be He.

────── Where Do You Think God Should Be in Our Priorities? ──────

The answer is that just as we are first in the Holy One's list of priorities, God wants and expects to be first in our list of priorities (in other words, subject to His will for everything in our lives). Only when the LORD is our first priority in life can we fully manifest the meaning of the following verse:

> **And God created the man in His own image, in the image of God He created him; male and female He created them. (Genesis 1:27)**

✦ The Hebrew word that is translated as image is צלם (*tzelem*). What is the meaning of this word here?

   a) Copy

   b) Image

   c) Reflection

   d) Shape

The answer is reflection. God wants humanity to reflect His characteristics in this world, as it is written in Isaiah:

> **Holy, holy, holy is the LORD of hosts; the whole earth is full of His glory! (Isaiah 6:3)**

It is important to know that this verse is part of the passage where the Holy One, blessed be He, calls Isaiah to serve Him, and from here we can arrive at the conclusion that the only way to fill the world with the glory of God is to serve Him. Only when we serve the Holy One can we reflect His attributes. This raises the question: How can we serve the Holy One?

Genesis chapter 2 provides a different perspective on the creation story, which gives us extra information about the creation of man, from which we learn about man and what the LORD expects from him. The chapter opens with the seventh day, when God rests from His work. In verse 7 we find extra information about the creation of man. While in chapter 1 the Torah uses the general word "ברא" (*bara*), which we translate as "created," in chapter 2 the Torah uses a different word:

> **The LORD God formed the man, dust from the ground and He breathed into his nostrils the spirit (breath) of life, and the man became a living being. (Genesis 2:7)**

According to our sages, the word "formed" (וַיִּיצֶר) refers to man in a special way. According to their interpretation, the fact that this word is spelled with two *yods* (י) hints at two creations: the creation of this world and the creation by means of the resurrection in the last days. Despite this, the animals which are not meant to stand in judgment, are not described using this word (see Rashi). Of course, the meaning of the two *yods* was conceived in the mind of the interpreter and is not Torah from heaven, yet at the same time, we can find a deep truth in the connection to Judgment Day. In addition, the Torah itself reveals that the Holy One formed man in a special way, as it is written: **"… and breathed into his nostrils the breath of life, and the man became a living being."** This personal and intimate action is what gave life to man, while these words are not used regarding the other creations. Why is this? Humanity is different from all other forms of life, and God wants to be in a personal relationship with man. From the New Covenant we learn that even though man was made to be a living creature, after the sin of the Tree of Knowledge, he was not in a condition to serve God. This is why it is written:

> **Therefore, Yeshua said to them again, "Peace to you. Just as the Father has sent Me, also I send you." And after saying this, He breathed and says to them, "Receive the Holy Spirit." (John 20:21–22)**

Just as the first man was dead until the Holy One breathed the breath of life into his nostrils, in the same way, this also is the state of every man, until he receives the gift of the Holy Spirit—he is considered spiritually dead.

In the next verses in chapter 2 of Genesis we see the Holy One give mankind a mission:

> **And the LORD God planted a garden in Eden, in the east, and He put there the man whom He had formed. And the LORD God made to spring up from the ground every tree that is pleasant**

> to the sight and good for food. And the tree of life in the midst
> of the garden, and the tree of the knowledge of good and evil.
> A river went out from Eden to water the garden, and from there
> it divided and became four heads (heads of rivers). The name of
> the first is the Pishon. It was around the whole land of Havilah,
> where there is gold. And gold of the land it is good; bdellium and
> onyx stone are there. And the name of the second river is Gihon.
> It was around the whole land of Cush. And the name of the third
> river is Tigris, which goes east of Assyria. And the fourth river is
> the Euphrates. The LORD God took the man and placed him in
> the garden of Eden to work it and keep it. (Genesis 2:8–15)

From this passage it can be learned that the Holy One provided Man with all of his needs and, in addition, assigned him with the task of working in the garden and protecting it. Afterward, God commanded man, as it is written:

> And the LORD God commanded the man, saying, "From every
> tree of the garden you may surely eat. But from the tree of the
> knowledge of good and evil you shall not eat from it, for in the
> day that you eat from it, you shall surely die." (Genesis 2:16–17)

As everyone knows, Adam and Eve did not abide by this commandment and sinned. As a result of this, they received the punishment about which the Holy One warned them: "For in the day that you eat of it you shall surely die." We can understand the concept of death in two ways:

a) Our relationship with God was impaired.

b) The human body started the process of aging, which ends in death.

According to the words of the Bible, the source of all of mankind is from the first man, and accordingly we were all born into this world in the same state as man after the sin of the Tree of Knowledge—disconnected from God (spiritually dead) and in need of salvation. A new question arises: according to Scripture, how can people find the path to salvation? The Apostle Shaul (Paul) taught us about the relationship between the creation of the world and salvation:

> For the wrath of God is revealed from heaven upon all ungodli-
> ness and unrighteousness of men; the truth, by unrighteousness
> was suppressed. Because (what is) known about God is manifest

> among them, for God, to them, has manifested. For His invisible attributes, from the creation of the world, by the things made, are known and clearly seen; by both His eternal power and divinity, for they are without excuse. For having known God, not as God did they glorify nor were they thankful; but they became vain in their rational thinking and was darkened, their foolish heart. (Romans 1:18–21)

In these verses, we see once again that God will judge mankind due to sin. What is sin? Shaul explains to the reader the idea of "sin" (which includes also the concepts of iniquity and trespassing) as every act, spoken word, or thought that is in contradiction with the Divine Truth, which is revealed solely through the Holy Scriptures (Hebrew Scriptures and the New Covenant only). As is known, not every person in the world has a copy of the Bible, and Paul speaks about this in the verses that we quoted from Romans. Even though not everyone owns a copy of the Bible, every person is supposed to know the reality of God through understanding the world that was created. Shaul continues and explains that from the moment that God's existence becomes clear to a person, he must seek Him. In the Proverbs, King Solomon says:

> I, those who love Me, love; and those who seek Me diligently, they will find Me. (Proverbs 8:17)

Let us study this verse carefully. The Word of the LORD teaches us that when one knows that God exists, he must love Him. In other words, the will to develop a relationship with God and to serve Him is bound together with searching after Him. This is the meaning of the word "מְשַׁחֲרַי" ("those who seek me," *meshacharai*), which comes from the root "שחר" (dawn, *shachar*), the first part of the day. We are all charged with the mission of making it first in our priorities in this life is to seek God with great effort. The verse ends with the expression "they will find Me," which means the Holy One promises that all those who seek Him will indeed find Him. From the quote in Romans it is clear to all that the Holy One will shine His light on those who seek Him in truth and sincerity, and to those who do not honor Him or give thanks to Him, He will cause "their foolish hearts [to be] ... darkened." In conclusion, the existence of God and His greatness need to be clear to any person from the act of creation alone, a fact that leaves no one with an excuse not to follow the Divine Truth.

Scripture clearly indicates that the Holy One charged the Messiah with the role of saving humanity. Consequently, it is important to understand that when someone begins to seek God out of a true desire to know Him in a personal way and to abide in His truth, he will come to the foregone conclusion that he is a sinner and in need of redemption, which he can ask for from the faithful God who will reveal to him the good news of the Messiah.

CHAPTER 1

1) How is it possible to know that your life is in need of correction by God?

2) What can give you the Spirit of the LORD?

3) What must you know before you can understand the meaning of life?

4) Many times in the Holy Scriptures, the Word of the LORD is likened to _____.

5) What is the only place that you can find the necessary information that reveals the will of God? _____.

6) In the Holy Scriptures light and darkness are likened to _____ and _____.

7) The special language used in Genesis regarding the first day of creation (day one) accentuates the _____ that the Holy One wants between Him and mankind.

8) God blessed and sanctified the Sabbath in order emphasize the importance of _____.

9) Knowing the will of God does not happen all at once, rather _____.

10) The words of the Torah regarding the Sabbath teach us that God should be our _____ priority.

11) Man can fill the world with the glory of the Holy One only when he _____ the will of the LORD.

12) God gave life to mankind in a different manner than any other creation when He _____.

13) The act of creation reveals that God wants a personal _____ with man.

14) Without the presence of the Spirit of the LORD within man, man is spiritually _____.

15) Every action, spoken word, and/or thought in contradiction with Divine Truth are
_____.

16) Creation reveals to all humanity that God wants a personal _____ with
mankind.

17) The LORD guaranteed every person that anyone who seeks God will also
_____ Him.

18) When a person finds God he wants to _____ Him.

19) It is a fact that every person was born after the first sin. When he sins personally against God, it reveals that every person is in need of redemption that
_____ alone can provide.

ANSWERS

1) There is no divine order in your life

2) Understanding

3) The Word of the LORD

4) Light

5) The Holy Scriptures

6) Good and Evil

7) Unity

8) The seventh day

9) Gradually

10) First

11) Reflects

12) Breathed into his nostrils the breath of life

13) Relationship

14) Dead

15) Sin

16) Relationship

17) Find

18) Serve

19) God

WHAT IS THE WORD OF GOD?
WHAT IS ITS IMPORTANCE?

When God created Adam He put him in the Garden of Eden, which is also called the Garden of God, a fact that points out the Holy One's desire to have a personal and close relationship with humanity. At the same time, it is not enough that man and God be in the same place in order to have a relationship; there is also a need for communication between them. As we know, without communication it is impossible to build a relationship, and this why the Holy One gave mankind His Word. In the Garden of Eden, God spoke with Adam and Eve directly, and later on the patriarchs also heard God's voice personally. Over time, we know that "Moses received the Torah from Sinai, and passed it to Joshua, and Joshua to the Elders, and the Elders to the Prophets" (*Pirkei Avot* 1:1), until finally the people of Israel had the Hebrew Scriptures (Tanach) in their possession. As believers and students of Yeshua the Messiah, we also receive the authority of the New Covenant as the Word of God. Therefore, when we use the expression "Holy Scriptures," we are referring to the Hebrew Scriptures and the New Covenant only. The purpose of this chapter is not to explain how the Word of God came to be, but rather to reveal the purpose of the Holy Scriptures and their usefulness for a believer. To accomplish this goal, we shall briefly look over what the Word of God testifies and teaches about itself.

Psalm 119, which is composed of 176 verses, deals entirely with the Word of God. Why specifically 176 verses? The answer is in the fact that 8 multiplied by 22 equals 176. There are 22 letters in the Hebrew alphabet and the number 8 has to do with redemption. (At the end of the book there is an appendix regarding numbers and their meanings).

✦ Meaning there is a direct relationship between the word of God to _____.

We can surely say that one of the main goals of the Word of God is to reveal to humanity the only way to be saved.

Earlier in the book we mentioned a well known verse from this psalm:

> **A lamp to my feet is Your Word, and a light to my path. (Psalm 119:105)**

We see the Word of God here as an important and beneficial tool that helps a believer to live according to the Holy One's will. From this verse we learn that the Holy Scriptures provide us with enlightenment, which is actually Divine Revelation meant to guide us. In other words, it is impossible for someone to obey God without a revelation that comes from His Word. Many times, various things in our lives interfere or prevent us from doing good deeds. Therefore it is important that every believer look inwardly and identify these things. King David related to this matter when he requested of God:

> **Search me, God, and know my heart! Test me and know my thoughts! And see if there be any grievous way in me, and lead me in the eternal (Kingdom) way. (Psalm 139: 23-24)**

It is important to point out that it would be difficult for any believer to understand the counsel of the Holy Spirit, when looking inward, without having a good understanding of the Word of God. This is because most of the time the Holy One speaks to us through His word.

In Judaism there is a tradition of searching for leaven on the night before Passover eve. Our sages determined that searching for leaven should be done specifically with a candle, and even today, when we have better light sources than candles, we still use candles. Why? Because the candle, with its limitations, forces us to check slowly and thoroughly, and only a small area at a time. This slow process causes the search for leaven to be precise and strict.

Shaul the Apostle also taught on this subject:

> **But you, continue in what you have learned and have believed, knowing from whom you learned and how from childhood you have known the sacred writings, the ones which are able to make you wise for salvation by means of faith in Messiah Yeshua. All Scripture is God-breathed and is profitable for teaching, for reproof, for correction, and for training in righteousness, in order that the man of God may be complete, being made equipped for every good work. (2 Timothy 3:14-17)**

In these passages we can find and recognize additional purposes of the Holy Scriptures: they were intended for instruction, to be used as a way of life, for rebuking sin and transgression, to indicate the upright path in the eyes of God, and to lead us in acts of justice before God.

Shaul says here that even young men (like Timothy) know and understand the advantages found in the Holy Scriptures, which give people wisdom regarding salvation and instruction on how to walk before the Holy One. It is important to internalize the relationship between the Word of God and salvation; through the Holy Scriptures, we can clearly see ourselves standing before the Holy One, which requires us to look at ourselves from God's perspective and understand that the LORD is holy while we are not, due to our sin. Likewise, through the Holy Scriptures we discover that the path to true redemption is by repenting through belief in the Messiah. It is important to note that the Holy Scriptures were formed under inspiration of the Holy Spirit, as it is written: **"Everything written was written in the Spirit of God."** We must emphasize, that in the original language, the literal meaning of the expression, "In the Spirit of God," is that the Holy One breathed His word into existence. The Hebrew רוח (*ruach*) means both spirit and breath. Accordingly, we understand that God gave those who wrote down His Word the necessary inspiration, that there would not be any sort of mistake in the biblical text, and that the Holy Scriptures truly are the Word of God. There is an additional aspect to the interpretation that the Holy One breathed His Word into existence, based in the story of the creation of man, as written in Genesis:

> **The LORD God formed the man, dust from the ground and breathed into his nostrils the breath (Spirit) of life, and the man became a living being. (Genesis 2:7)**

The quintessential point that comes up from this passage is that man cannot live a physical life without the breath of life; without the Word of God it is impossible for mankind to live a spiritual life according to God's will.

What is the goal of the Word of God? According to Shaul the Apostle, the answer is that **"the man of God may be complete, being made equipped for every good work."** Since mankind was created in order to reflect the LORD's majesty, it is very important that we engage in good deeds as described in Scripture. The Judaism with which we are familiar today is a rabbinical Judaism that is based upon rabbinic literature and traditions whose sources are from human beings. In *yeshivas*, the main thing that is studied is the Talmud and the Shulchan Aruch. How do you think Yeshua would react to this reality? In His time, when one Pharisee asked Yeshua about the tradition of the elders (the foundation of rabbinic literature), Yeshua answered and said:

> For leaving the commandment of God and you hold to the tradi-
> tion of men. (Mark 7:8)

From Yeshua's words it is completely clear that there is a contradiction between the
LORD's commandments and rabbinic literature, in such a way that when someone
chooses to walk more according to the tradition of the elders than according to
the the the commandments of the LORD, the result is that he actually leaves the divine
framework. As we know, the rabbis refuse to accept the New Covenant; however,
according to Yeshua:

> But He answered, "It is written, 'Not by bread alone will man
> live, but by every word that comes from the mouth of God.'"
> (Matthew 4:4)

It is important to note that we do not see the tradition of the elders as something
bad or invalid, as long as it does not contradict the Word of God. Many people give
the same weight to the tradition of the elders and the Scriptures, which can cause
distancing from the Holy One, blessed be He.

Yeshua knew that the Holy Scriptures have supernatural power. As we have already
learned, there is a connection between the Word of God and salvation (redemption),
and as such it needs to be clear that in order to enter the Kingdom of God we must
be saved. When Yeshua spoke with one of the leaders of the Sanhedrin, named Nico-
demus He told him the following regarding the Kingdom of Heaven:

> Yeshua answered and said to him, "Truly, truly, I say to you, un-
> less one is born from above he cannot see the kingdom of God."
> (John 3:3)

This verse is interesting in several ways, one of which is the expression "born from
above." The commentators agree that this expression describes supernatural activity
that happens in the life of a man who is saved (redeemed). As we have already seen,
through the Torah we learn the Holy One's expectations from humanity and the need
to be saved. A question now arises: Where can we learn to be saved? The disciple
Shimon (Simon Peter) answers this question:

> Have been born again, not of perishable seed but of imperishable,
> through the living and abiding forever Word of God. (1 Peter 1:23)

Though it is written "born again," it is important to note that the same word that appears in this passage is what we have read before in the Gospel according to Yochanan (John). That is, the second birth is the birth from above. The passive form of the word "born" that Shimon used is very meaningful, since the passive reveals that another Power (and not the person himself) caused him to *be born* again. Of course, this birth is different from the first. What exactly causes this? The answer is the Word of God, as it is written: **"The living and abiding forever Word of God."** With these words Shimon reveals that beyond the fact that the Holy Scriptures are the source of salvation, the Word of God is living and enduring forever!

What does Shimon mean when he says that the Word of the LORD is living? There are two possible interpretations. The first has to do with the expression "born from above," meaning, the Word of God gives life to humanity. The other interpretation is that the Word of the LORD is something living (not inanimate). Yochanan's words in the following passages affirm what is written in Isaiah 9:7:

> **In the beginning was the Word, and the Word was with God, and God was the Word. (John 1:1)**

> **And the Word became flesh and dwelt among us, and we perceived His glory, glory as of the only Begotten from the Father, full of grace and truth. (John 1:14)**

These two passages show the close relationship between the Holy Scriptures and Yeshua. According to them, Yeshua reflects perfectly the essence of the Word of the LORD. This is the reason that it is written over and over again in the New Covenant regarding Yeshua's deeds: **"For these things took place that the Scripture might be fulfilled."**

It is important to clarify that when the New Covenant refers to Scripture, it is referring to the Hebrew Scriptures (Tanach). One time Yeshua spoke with several of Israel's leaders regarding the Old Testament and said to them:

> **You search the Scriptures because you think in them you have eternal life; and it is they that bear witness concerning Me. (John 5:39)**

This verse reveals an important matter in the writings of the sages. It is a well-known fact that the Word of God teaches the reader about eternal life, that is, the final redemption. Yeshua says here that the leaders who investigate the Scriptures and search for information on this subject should be able to recognize Him, because Scripture testifies to Him. But the fact that they acted against Him reveals to us that their method of interpreting Scripture is wrong.

Scripture can be seen as a gradual revelation from the Holy One over time, so that all later revelation is based on the revelations that preceded it. Theologians speak of revelation as a process and therefore use the term "progressive revelation." It is important to understand that a new revelation must be complementary and by no means contradictory. Yeshua Himself is the source of revelation, as written about Him:

> Long ago, at many times and in many ways, God has spoken to our fathers by the prophets, but in these last days He has spoken to us by His Son, whom He appointed heir of all things, through Whom also He made the ages. He is the radiance of the glory of God and the exact expression of His essence, and He upholds all things by the word of His power. Through Himself (is the) purification of our sins, He sat down at the right hand of the Majesty on high. (Hebrews 1:1–3)

From these verses, we can learn that beyond the fact that Yeshua is the source of revelation, He Himself is also the image of the essence of God. This does not mean that the prophets and the other authors of the Bible constitute lesser revelation than that of Yeshua; rather, despite the fact that all Scripture is on the same level, the things that Yeshua taught, provide the reader with the framework through which the rest of the Scriptures can be interpreted and explained more precisely. On the basis of this fact, students of the Bible can conclude that the best interpreter of the Word of the LORD is the Word of the LORD Himself. This is why Shimon the Apostle said:

> This first, knowing that all prophecy of Scripture, is not of one's own interpretation. For not by the will of man was prophecy brought forth, but by the Holy Spirit it was brought forth, holy men of God spoke. (2 Peter 1:20–21)

These verses teach us that it is impossible to write even one word of the Holy Scriptures without the inspiration of the Holy Spirit. Likewise, in order to interpret the Word of God in the right manner, every person needs the Holy Spirit. The Prophet Isaiah also spoke about the same matter when he said:

> For not My thoughts are your thoughts, neither are your ways My ways, declares the LORD. For heavens are higher than the earth, Yes, are higher My ways higher than your ways and My thoughts than your thoughts. (Isaiah 55:8–9)

✸ Since the Word of the LORD came to be by the inspiration of the Holy Spirit, it can be said confidently that in the Holy Scriptures there are no:

a) Information about science

b) Advice for a person today

c) **Mistakes**

d) Anything related to unholy things

Every believer in Yeshua must accept the authority of the Holy Scriptures. This means to accept the fact that there are no mistakes in the Scriptures in their original versions (meaning before the copies that came from scribes throughout the years). It can certainly be known that the Holy Scriptures are the word of truth, since the Word of the LORD came to be through the inspiration of the Holy Spirit. When a person refuses to accept this truth, it has terrible, negative implications for that person. One of them is that he places himself in the position to decide what in the Word of the LORD is true and what is not true. Of course, the risk here is that only things that make sense to him will be accepted in his eyes as truth, while the things that he does not like he will refuse to accept.

✸ So far we have learned that the Word of the LORD is:

a) Supernatural

b) Full of inspiration from the Holy Spirit

c) Without mistakes

d) Authoritative

e) Relevant to every area of life

f) **All answers are correct**

In light of all these things, we must implement the Word of God in our lives. As the author of the letter to the Hebrews said:

> For Living is the Word of God and active, sharper than any two-edged sword, and penetrating unto (the) division of soul and of spirit, of joints and of marrow, and judging the thoughts and intentions of the heart. (Hebrews 4:12)

When a person is saved, he becomes a new creation, yet that does not mean he is perfect. There is a big difference between salvation and sanctification. Although we will study these two issues in depth later, we should now define the relationship between God's Word and the concept of sanctification. The verse we quoted reveals to the reader that the Scriptures are the most powerful tool to help the believer progress on the path to holiness. It is important to understand that salvation gives a believer the ability to enter the Kingdom of God by merit of the Holy One's lovingkindness; however, as long as the believer is in the physical body, the possibility and ability to advance toward holiness (the goal) is given him by the instruction of the Holy Spirit and God's Word.

Every believer must understand how the Holy Spirit works together with God's word in order to cause the believer to grow in faith. The first thing that was said in the above verse about God's word is that it is living and active. This means, when a believer reads Scripture he is not only learning what is written in it as in any other book, but also bringing into himself a great and supernatural (spiritual) power that acts upon all parts of man (body, soul, spirit, and the subconscious).

The first letter of Shimon says:

> **As newborn babies, spiritual (from the mind of God) pure milk, in order that by it, you may be made to mature for salvation; if you have tasted (that) the Lord (is) good. (1 Peter 2:2–3)**

Shimon wants to tell us that just as a baby needs his mother's milk in order for him to live, exist, and grow, so too, we must relate to the Word of God.

There are those who limit what God's Word can do in our lives due to a mistaken thought that Scripture can affect man only when he reads it or hears another person reading it out loud. God's Word is meant to act in our lives at any given moment so that we can walk according to the Holy One's will:

> **In my heart, I have hidden your word, so that I might not sin against You. (Psalm 119:11)**

We must understand that one of the central roles of the Holy Scriptures in our life comes from their name—the *Holy* Scriptures. We must strive to walk in *holiness* and sanctity before God, according to His Word, day by day. The Apostle Shaul says about God's Word:

> That he might sanctify her, having cleansed by the washing of
> water in the word. (Ephesians 5:26)

The context of the quote is the relationship between a man and a wife. Shaul compared this love to the relationship between Messiah Yeshua and our community. In the next verse it says that in the end His bride will be perfect:

> In order that He might present to Himself in glory the community, not having spot or wrinkle or any such thing, but in order that she should be holy and without blemish. (Ephesians 5:27)

How did the community get to this situation? The answer is found in verse 26: **"That He might sanctify her with His word."** It is important to note that in the original language the words **"cleansed by the washing of water"** have to do with His Word (Scripture). Likewise, another translation can be read: **"In order to sanctify and purify her by the washing of water accompanied by His word."** The main message is the washing of water, the immersion in water, which is learning God's Word, by which the student advances in his spiritual journey and grows and matures until he becomes holy, without spot or blemish.

Our lives are holy because our Creator is holy. Our purpose is to strive to a life of holiness according to the LORD's will. At the same time, it is important to note that in order to be holy without spot or blemish, we must understand that our desire to arrive to divine holiness will not bring us to the world of salvation. Nevertheless, the result of redemption in the believer's life is that the Holy Spirit lives and dwells within us, and accordingly we must strive to a life of holiness and rid ourselves of any impurity.

> My son, if you receive my words and my commandments you
> will hide within you, making your ear to listen to wisdom and
> inclining your heart to understanding; for if for insight you
> will call out, for discernment you will give your voice, if you
> will seek it like silver and as for hidden treasures you will
> search for it, then you will understand the fear of the LORD and
> the knowledge of God you will find. (Proverbs 2:1–5)

In order to understand and know the true will of God in our lives, it is not enough to only read God's Word, but we must learn it and delve into it. In order to know what God's Word means in each and every topic, we must also learn the proper way to interpret Scripture. It is not the goal of this book to dive into this topic, but it is important for us to challenge the reader and give a couple of points that will help us all to know and understand God's Word and will. The LORD did not give us His Word to confuse us, rather He gave it so that we would interpret His Word according to the plain reading. Of course, there are plenty of proverbs and allegories in the Bible, but most of the time it is very easy to identify and understand them, and often the text itself gives the reader the correct interpretation. It is very important to pay attention to the words that appear in Scripture and how those words are used in different places in the Bible. Additionally, the student must learn the background, culture of the place, and the time period of what is being recounted.

CHAPTER 2

1) Throughout history, the Holy One has shown His will to be in a _____ with humanity.

2) _____ is the main source in which Divine Revelation can be found.

3) Anyone who studies the Scriptures understands that he:

   a) Will be in the Kingdom of God

   b) Will find favor in God's eyes

   c) Is meant to be honored

   d) Is a sinner

4) God's Word comes to be through _____.

5) Without the Scriptures, every person is:

   a) Free to do as he pleases

   b) Required to listen to other to others that seem more spiritual than him

   c) Spiritually dead

   d) Not committed to doing good deeds

6) In order to enter God's Kingdom, you must be _____ from above.

7) There is a special connection between God's Word and His _____.

8) According to John 5:39, the leaders of the people of Israel who lived two thousand years ago knew how to properly interpret Scripture.

   a) True

   b) False

9) God's Word testifies that Messiah:

   a) Is temporary

   b) Will not die

   c) Is created

   d) Is Yeshua

10) The best interpretation of Scripture is found in:

   a) Rashi

b) The Scriptures

c) Rambam

d) Academic papers

11) God's Word is written in the inspiration of:

a) Rashi

b) The Holy Spirit

c) Rambam

12) When someone reads Scripture, it affects his:

a) Brain

b) Subconscious

c) Soul

d) Spirit

e) All of the above

13) God's Word can affect someone only while he is reading or thinking about it.

a) True

b) False

14) When someone learns God's Word, it is important that he pay attention to:

a) The wording of the Bible

b) The background

c) The context

d) All of the above

ANSWERS

1) Relationship

2) Scripture

3) D

4) Inspiration of the Holy Spirit

5) C

6) Born

7) Will

8) False

9) D

10) B

11) B

12) E

13) False

14) D

THE HOLY ONE, BLESSED BE HE

King David said: **"Oh, taste and see that the LORD is good! Blessed is the man who takes refuge in Him"** (Psalm 34:9). It is important to notice that before David said the words: **"Blessed is the man who takes refuge in Him,"** he invites everyone to learn about God personally. This is the purpose of this verse: to invite you to learn about the one and only God who is revealed by the Scriptures. Instead of the phrase "to learn about," it is better to use the word "know," since the purpose is not to just to know things *about* God. In other words, we want more than just to know that God exists. We want to *know* God, to know Him personally. The first word in that verse is "taste." As we know, there is a big difference between someone who has heard that a certain restaurant has good food, and someone else who is dining in that restaurant and eating its delicacies.

God wants each of us to know Him through a special relationship called a "covenant." The term covenant refers to the framework defined by God's word, and that gives us the conditions that this relationship is based upon. God reveals Himself through two main media: through creation and through the Holy Scriptures. Accordingly, even if someone does not have a personal copy of God's Word, it is a clear fact that the world exists and is managed by someone. Anyone can see that the world is not in a state of chaos and void; if so, who manages it in such an organized way? The answer, of course, is God. After we understand that God exists, we must seek Him. In other words, every person should want to take on King David's invitation: **"Taste and see that the LORD is good!"**

✸ It is better to *know* God than to just *know about* Him. The Hebrew word "לדעת" means:

    a) Personal knowledge

    b) Personal experience

    c) Relationship

    d) All answers are correct

In the first verse in the BIble we read: **"In the beginning God (אלהים, *Elohim*) created the Heavens and the Earth."** Before we speak about the LORD as the Creator of the Universe, we need to pay attention to how this verse refers to the LORD. The first word referring to God in the Bible is *Elohim*, which we generally translate as "God." What is the meaning of *Elohim*?

According to our sages, the answer is "judge." This meaning is based on the verse:

> **God stands in the divine council; in the midst of gods, He will judge. (Psalm 82:1)**

The Torah says that God created the world to reveal to the reader that He will also judge the world. Since God is to judge all of creation, He will also judge you. Accordingly, it makes sense that each of us would want to know his or her Judge. The first thing we must know about God is the nature of His relationship to creation. When we use gematria, the words *Elohim* and *ha'teva* (הטבע, "nature") have the same numerical value—86.

אלהים = 1 + 30 + 5 + 10 + 40 = 86

הטבע = 5 + 9 + 2 + 70 = 86

Those who deal with gematria see a connection between God and the creation of the world due to the identical value of these two words. We, as disciples of Yeshua, do not use gematria at all, and do not base our beliefs off of it. Judaism in general, and especially Chasidic Judaism, claim that in each and every person there is part of the Holy One or, in other words, the entire creation is God. This sentence is heresy!

According to the fact that the Holy One created everything, there is a separation between God and creation. It is a big mistake to say that everything created is part of Him. In order to justify Judaism's claim that everything is part of Him, the rabbis quote the following verse:

> **To you it was shown, to know that the LORD is God; there is no other besides Him. (Deuteronomy 4:35)**

The second part of this sentence that states "there is no other besides Him" can also be read as "there is nothing except for Him." They put the emphasis on this part of the verse and their intention is that there is nothing else besides God in the universe. The problem with this interpretation is that this verse does not refer to creation, but to the fact that the God of Israel alone is the only God. As stated earlier, it is a mistake to say that God put part of Himself in everything that He created, though there most certainly is a special connection between God and creation. There are a few things that can be said about this connection:

a) Everything that exists was created by the Holy One alone.

> **Because in Him all things were created, in the heavens and on the earth, visible and invisible, whether thrones whether dominions whether rulers whether authorities—all things through Him and for Him they were created. (Colossians 1:16)**

b) God acts within His creation to a certain extent.

> **That His Sun He makes to rise on evil and good, and sends rain on just and unjust. (Matthew 5:45)**

> **Good is the LORD to all, and His mercy is over all His deeds. (Psalm 145:9)**

c) God is omnipresent in his Creation.

> **Where shall I go from Your Spirit? And where from before Your presence shall I flee? If I ascend to heaven, there You are! And (if) I make my bed in Sheol, Behold You (are there)! (Psalm 139:7–8)**

From these three points we learn that God did not just create the world and ignore it, rather, He knows perfectly about everything taking place in the universe:

> **Are not two sparrows for a penny sold? And one of them will not fall to the ground apart from your Father. And you even the hairs of your head are all numbered. (Matthew 10:29–30)**

Even though God knows His creation perfectly and acts within it, we must understand that this fact is only part of God's greatness, meaning that His greatness is beyond creation. The name Y-H-V-H (י–ה–ו–ה) is based on the root of verb "to be" (להיות). The name above all names is made up of three words: *was* (היה), *is* (הווה), and *will be* (יהיה). This indicates that God is not limited by the fabric of space and time. When we study the Scriptures about God we learn a lot about His qualities. The fact that we are human beings and limited in our ability to know the fullness of God is not in contradiction to the fact that we must try to learn as much as possible about God through His Word.

One of the terms used by the rabbis to describe God is the *Ein Sof* (without end). This term, reflects several aspects. First, God is eternal. In other words, there was no time in which God did not exist. God is not only before everything, but He also has no beginning or end. Secondly, as we have already noted, God is not limited by the fabric of time and space. It is important to note here that God will not do anything contrary to His character. For example, if it is written that God cannot lie (see Numbers 23:19), the fact that God does not lie does not imply any limitation. God simply does nothing against His will and essence.

The Prophet Ezekiel says:

> **Do I desire (the) death of the wicked, declares the Lord GOD;**
> **rather that he should turn from his way and live? (Ezekiel 18:23)**

From this verse, it is clear that God wants every person to repent and live (to be saved), but we know that not every person chooses to do so. Does this fact harm the sovereignty of God? Absolutely not! We must distinguish between God's desires and His will. Everything that is in God's will to do He does and fulfills, but what God commands humanity to do is given to free will. Accordingly, we must not blame God for man's sins or think that there is a violation of his sovereignty since people sin. The LORD is the one who created the framework which allows humanity to choose between good and evil.

There are four important things to remember about God:

a) God is omnipresent.

b) God is omniscient.

c) God is omnipotent.

d) The LORD, the God of Israel, is the only God.

Regarding these four points and any other matter that pertains to His essence, we must know and remember that God does not change:

> **In a more abundant manner God desired to show more to the**
> **heirs of the promise the unchangeable character of His pur-**
> **pose, He guaranteed with an oath, in order that by two un-**
> **changeable things, in which it is impossible for God to lie, strong**

> encouragement we have the one who have fled for refuge, to take
> hold of hope having been set before. (Hebrews 6:17–18)

Since God does not change or lie, He is absolutely faithful:

> And you will Know that the LORD your God He is the God, the
> faithful God, He keeps covenant and the grace to those who love
> him and keep His commandments, to a thousand generations.
> (Deuteronomy 7:9)

Although God commands mankind to obey Him, that does not mean He needs anything. Every commandment is for our benefit and not for His benefit. God is not dependent upon others; there is a strong connection between the fact that God is not limited and the fact that He does not depend on anything. As it is written in Psalms:

> And our God is in the heavens; all which He desires, He does.
> (Psalm 115:3)

Various words can be used to describe God, but there is a small group of adjectives that often appear in relation to God's attributes. This list includes the words: holy, righteous, true, and good. We should note that there is no word in this list related to the fact that God has attributes that testify to His grace. We will deal with the grace of God at the end of this chapter. It must be understood that there is a connection between the four words: holy, righteous, true, and good. But before we explore this connection, it is important to understand that God is not defined by these words; on the contrary, the essence of God is what defines these terms. In other words, it is not correct to say that the LORD is righteous because He does righteous deeds, but that something is an act of justice because God did so. Every adjective that is appropriate for God suits Him because this is God's essence.

In general, the term "holy" refers to a specific plan or purpose. Something becomes "holy" when it is dedicated to a particular purpose. For example, a knife can be used for any purpose, but when someone dedicates the knife to a specific purpose, it can be said that the knife is now "holy". However, it is important to understand that we are talking about the term "holy" in general only and not spiritually (the common context in which this word is used today). Here is an example to help us understand the meaning of "holy" in two contexts: So and so is a criminal who has lots of money. He takes $500 of his money and buys a gun to rob a bank. In general we can say that those $500 are "holy" or "set apart." Of course, spiritually there is nothing holy about money, since in this instance it is in connection with sin. For something to be spiritually sacred, the plan or purpose for which it is dedicated must be on the same page with the will of God.

In the Torah it is written "Holy am I, the LORD your God." As we saw before, God is holy in His essence, but additionally, this verse shows the reader that God is holy, meaning God is loyal to His own will (His plan). In the same verse we read:

> **Speak to all the congregation of the Sons of Israel and say to them, holy ones you shall be, for holy am I the LORD your God.** (**Leviticus 19:2**)

According to this verse, God invited the children of Israel to join His plan. It is important to note that this plan (God's will) is based on truth, and that God Himself defines truth [**"The LORD is the God of truth"** (Psalm 31:6)].

The connection between the concepts "truth" and "good" can now be seen. The first time the word "good" appears in Scripture is in Genesis 1:4. From this verse and others, in which this word appears, we learn that the meaning of "good" is "according to the will of God." Truth always describes the good and is based on the divine plan.

God is righteous, as it is written: **"I am the LORD and there is no god besides Me, righteous God and Savior; there is none other than Me"** (Isaiah 45:21). The term "justice" can be defined as "the result of God's will." For example: There is a trial and there is a just trial, but it is clear to all that a just trial is one which expresses God's will. The expression "God is righteous" says that God will always act so that His perfect and just will may be manifested.

Here is another example that will help us understand the four words: holy, righteous, true, and good.

God wants to establish His Kingdom from Jerusalem. Therefore, it can be understood that Jerusalem is a holy city because God dedicated it to the plan to establish His Kingdom. Since the plan to establish the Kingdom in Jerusalem is in accordance with the will of God, it can be said that it is a *good* thing. Therefore, anything that describes this plan in the right way is *true*, and anything that is done to advance that plan is an act of justice.

The city of Jerusalem is _____.

Due to God's desire to establish His Kingdom therein, He is _____.

Everything that accurately describes His Kingdom is _____.

All that is done to advance His plan is a _____ act.

Answers: Holy / Righteous / True / Good

God's Grace

Our sages spoke about thirteen attributes of mercy found in the Torah:

> **The LORD passed before him and proclaimed, "The LORD, the LORD, God is merciful and gracious, slow to anger, and abounding in grace and truth, keeping grace for thousands, forgiving iniquity and transgression and sin, and Who cleans and does not clean, visiting the iniquity of the fathers on the children and the children's children, to the third and the fourth (generation)." (Exodus 34:6–8)**

They divided these verses as follows:

a) LORD

b) LORD

c) God

d) Merciful

e) Gracious

f) Slow to anger

g) Abounding in grace

h) Faithfulness

i) Keeping grace for thousands

j) Forgiving iniquity

k) Forgiving transgression

l) Forgiving sin

m) And cleaning (the guilty)

As believers, disciples of Yeshua, we are not under the authority of the sages, and we are entitled to disagree with their interpretation, but it is clear that these two verses are connected to the grace of God. Although, according to the sages' interpretation there are thirteen references to the grace of God, from the reading of the verses one can clearly see seven references to this matter: merciful, gracious, slow to anger, abounding in grace and faithfulness, keeping grace for thousands, forgiving iniquity and transgression and sin, and cleaning, and not cleaning. Merciful, gracious, and abounding in grace and faithfulness express His divine attributes. The phrase "slow to anger" reveals to the reader that God has patience and so He gives us time to repent. The rest of the points refer to God's deeds: keeping grace for thousands, forgiving iniquity and transgression and sin, and cleaning, that we may be able to receive His forgiveness.

We must rejoice in the fact that God wants to forgive sinners, but because He is holy and righteous we must remember that God will punish those who refuse His grace. It is important to note that it is not coincidental that the word "truth" appears in the above passage to teach us that God will forgive, but only under His conditions, as it appears in God's Word. If any person does not meet these conditions, God will judge him in a just trial. There are those who think that since it is written, **"God is love"** (1 John 4:8), in the end God will forgive everyone; but one must not ignore the fact that according to Scripture, God is also a God of jealousy and wrath:

> **For you shall not worship a different god, for the LORD, Jealous is His name, a jealous God He is! (Exodus 34:14)**

> **For the LORD your God is a consuming fire, He is a jealous God. (Deuteronomy 4:24)**

> **He sent among them His burning anger, wrath, indignation, and distress, a delegation of evil angels. (Psalm 78:49)**

> **And Israel joined to Baal Peor. And the anger of the LORD was kindled against Israel. (Numbers 25:3)**

CHAPTER 3

1) In order for us to respond to God correctly we must first _____ Him.

2) What is the meaning of the word "*Elohim*"?

   a) Lord

   b) Infinite

   c) Judge

   d) Creator of the World

3) All nature put together equals God.

   a) True

   b) False

4) What is the meaning of the phrase in the Torah "there is none besides Him"?

   a) God is everything

   b) God put part of Himself in everything that He created

   c) Everything created is essentially divine

   d) There are no other gods besides Him

5) God is everywhere in the universe.

   a) True

   b) False

6) It is possible that something can happen in the world and God will not know about it until it happens.

   a) True

   b) False

7) The name Y-H-V-H reveals to us that God isn't bound by _____.

   a) Knowledge

   b) Time

   c) Space

   d) Rage

8) Something sacred was sanctified for a certain _____ .

    a) Plan

    b) Purpose

    c) Both a and b

    d) No correct answer

9) God is righteous only because He does righteous deeds.

    a) True

    b) False

10) Truth has nothing to do with God's will.

    a) True

    b) False

11) The fact that God is love contradicts:

    a) God's wrath

    b) God's justice

    c) The need for Hell

    d) No correct answer

12) The phrase "slow to anger" refers to:

    a) God's zeal

    b) God's wrath

    c) God's patience

    d) All of the above

ANSWERS

1) Know

2) C

3) False

4) D

5) True

6) False

7) B

8) C

9) False

10) False

11) D

12) C

THE MESSIAH, THE SON OF GOD

In the first verse of the Gospel of Mark, Yeshua is called the Son of God. Even when Yeshua stood before the Sanhedrin, toward the end of His life, Caiaphas, the high priest, asked Him: **"Are you (the Messiah) the Son of God?"** (Luke 22:70). What does "Son of God" mean? The answer is found in the high priest's response to Yeshua's positive answer:

> And the high priest tore his garments and says, "What, we still need witnesses? You have heard His blasphemy. What does it appear to you?" And they all condemned Him to be deserving death. (Mark 14:63–64)

The high priest tore his clothes not because Yeshua said that the Messiah is God, but because He said about Himself that He is the Messiah. This represents a significant difference to the sages today. According to the rabbis, the Messiah is only flesh and blood and not essentially divine. Despite this being the common view in Judaism today, the fact that the high priest asked Yeshua if He was the Messiah, the Son of God, reveals to the reader that two thousand years ago the great rabbis of Israel indeed understood and interpreted that the Messiah is divine.

✦ The fact that Caiaphas, the high priest did not ask Yeshua if He is the Messiah, but if He was the Messiah, the Son of God, reveals that two thousand years ago the great rabbis of Israel thought that the Messiah is:

a) Flesh and blood

b) An angel

c) Chose by Sanhedrin

d) **Divine**

It is important that we understand Yeshua's answer to this question:

> And Yeshua said, "I am, and you will see the Son of Man sitting at
> the right hand of Power, and coming with the clouds of heaven."
> (Mark 14:62)

Yeshua is not just a man, but he is also the Son of God. Additionally, He also quoted Daniel in order to teach Caiaphas and the rest of the Sanhedrin about this matter. The book of Daniel contains one of the most important testimonies that reveals that the Messiah is divine:

> I saw in the night visions, and behold, with the clouds of heaven,
> One like a son of man, and He came to the Ancient of Days and
> was presented before Him. And to Him was given dominion and
> honor and a kingdom, that all peoples, nations, and languages will
> serve (worship) Him; His dominion is an everlasting dominion,
> which shall not pass away, and His kingdom one that shall not be
> destroyed. (Daniel 7:13–14)

In verse 13, the Messiah—the Son of Man—appeared in heaven and approached the Ancient of Days—God Himself. In the next verse we read that the Messiah received "dominion and honor and a Kingdom" and as such all peoples, nations, and languages must serve, i.e. worship Him. The sages interpret that the meaning of יפלחון (literally, "to worship") as "to serve," and that this does not have to do with the worship of LORD. The obvious question is: Were the sages right?

These verses are very important in order to understand the Messiah's true identity. There is no argument in Judaism regarding the fact that the Messiah is a human being. The problem that arises from the verse that we quoted from the book of Daniel is that **"all peoples, nations, and languages will worship Him."** If the Messiah is only flesh and blood, then when all nations worship Him, it would be considered idol worship. The sages argue that it is wrong to translate יפלחון as the worship of God, but rather as a person who is serving his master or king. Are the sages right in this case? In order to answer this question, we must first research how Daniel used the root of this word "פלח" in other contexts in Aramaic. This Aramaic root appears a few other times in the book of Daniel, and each time it is quite clear that the intention is the worship of God. Here are a few examples:

> There are certain Jews whom you have appointed over the affairs
> of the province of Babylon: Shadrach, Meshach, and Abednego.

> These men, O king, pay no attention to you; they do not *serve* (פלחין) your gods or worship the golden image that you have set up. (Daniel 3:12)

> Nebuchadnezzar answered and said to them, "Is it true, O Shadrach, Meshach, and Abednego, that you do not *serve* my gods or worship the golden image that I have set up?" (Daniel 3:14)

> Shadrach, Meshach, and Abednego answered and said to the king, "O Nebuchadnezzar, we have no need to answer you in this matter. If this be so, our God whom we *serve* is able to deliver us from the burning fiery furnace, and He will deliver us out of your hand, O king. But if not, be it known to you, O king, that we will not *serve* your gods or worship the golden image that you have set up." (Daniel 3:17–18)

In all these verses, the service being referred is divine service, whether to the one true God or to Nebuchadnezzar's false gods. Therefore, when Daniel speaks of the Messiah in the same book as the above verses, it is clear that the nations will, in fact, **worship** the Messiah.

There are two possible reasons why the sages chose not to give the root "פ-ל-ח" the meaning of "to praise, extol, glorify, elevate, glorify, bless, and raise up" (see the prayer *Shochen Ad* from the Sabbath morning prayers):

a) The sages did not have the right way to interpret the Scriptures.

b) The sages purposely choose to misinterpret this verb in order to hide from the Jewish readers the meaning of the "Son of God."

It is important to emphasize that the sages intentionally hid the correct definition of this word, even though they knew well that when someone wants to know the meaning of a certain word, he must check its other uses in the Bible, especially in the same book, in one of the only places where Aramaic is used. When researching the meaning of the root "פ-ל-ח" only one conclusion can be arrived at, that this word only means serving God. For this reason we claim that the sages concealed the correct meaning of this word.

✱ Daniel taught that when someone worships the Messiah, like when worshiping God, he is:

a) Sinning in idol worship

b) **Behaving properly**

c) Doing an unforgivable sin

d) No correct answer

Man is allowed to worship Messiah only if He is "the Son of God," and this will not be considered a sin of idolatry. The concept of "the Son of God" is completely alien to today's Judaism, but the important question arises: Is this concept justified in the Bible?

The answer is yes.

In addition to the book of Daniel, the Prophet Isaiah also spoke of the Son of God saying:

> For a Child is born for us, a Son is given to us; and the government will be upon His shoulder, and His name will be called Wonderful Counselor, Mighty God, Everlasting Father, Prince of Peace. (Isaiah 9:5)

From these verses we can learn that Yeshua is a human being in the full sense of the word, and also a divine being (the Son of God). One of the things that points to this is the way in which Miriam, the mother of Yeshua, became pregnant, something which is related to his identity and essence.

We read in the Gospels that Miriam became pregnant by the Holy Spirit:

> And the angel said to her, "Do not be afraid, Miriam, for you have found grace from God. And behold, you will conceive in your womb and bear a Son, and you will call His name Yeshua. This One will be great and will be called the Son of the Most High. And the Lord God will give to Him the Throne of His father David, and He will reign over the house of Jacob forever, and of His kingdom there will be no end." But Miriam said to the angel, "How will this be, since a man I have not known?" And the angel answered her, "The Holy Spirit will come upon you, and the power of the Most High will overshadow you; therefore the Holy One being born from you will be called the Son of God." (Luke 1:30–35)

> And the birth of Yeshua the Messiah was thusly. For His mother Miriam had been betrothed to Yoseph, before they came to-gether was found having in the womb (One) from the Holy Spirit. (Matthew 1:18)

The birth of Yeshua from the virgin reveals how God put on flesh and came into this world to redeem humanity (those who accept Him). When we speak of the birth of Yeshua from a virgin, it is important to emphasize that although the virgin became pregnant she remained a virgin until Yeshua's birth. There is a reason why Miriam conceived not by human sperm. In Jeremiah's prophecy it is written:

> Thus said the LORD: "Write this man down as childless, a man who will not succeed in his days; for not will succeed from his offspring, one sitting on the throne of David and ruling again in Judah." (Jeremiah 22:30)

Who does this verse speak of? The answer is Jehoiachin, the king of Judah, who was a very bad king. Jeremiah prophesied that Jehoiachin would not have a son who would rule over the throne of David, so the Messiah could not be a biological descendant of Jehoiachin, which is very problematic since in the genealogy of Yeshua of Nazareth, which appears in the Gospel of Matthew, contains the name of Jehoiachin.

Ostensibly, this would have prevented Yeshua from being a "nominee" for the role of Messiah and, in addition, since that prophecy was given, the genealogy of the Messiah is cut off. There is only one solution: the Messiah must be of the lineage of the kings of Judah legally (not adopted), but cannot be a biological descendant of Jehoiachin. This solution seems at first impossible; however, the only way to implement it is that a woman married to a man from the house of David was pregnant without human seed. Only this way could the Messiah come. This is why it is so important that the Messiah was born of a virgin.

So far we have learned that the Messiah is a human, but also a divine being in every sense. Shaul the Apostle also wrote these two principles:

> The first man from the earth, made of dust; the second man, The LORD from heaven. (1 Corinthians 15:47)

From this verse we see that Shaul taught that Yeshua, "the Second Man," is truly a human, but His origin was from heaven. Yeshua left heaven and put on flesh in order to do His intended service, as it is written:

> **For one God, one also Mediator of God and of men, the Man Messiah Yeshua. (1 Timothy 2:5)**

To be a mediator, Yeshua had to be a real person. However, the fact that Yeshua was flesh and blood fulfills only part of His role, while the second part of His role as mediator is related to His divinity. Shaul wrote about this:

> **That in Him, He was pleased, all the fullness to dwell. (Colossians 1:19)**

Shaul's intention for this verse is that in Yeshua, God was pleased that all of His fullness (His Divinity) dwelt. Saul taught the same thing when he said elsewhere:

> **Who, in the form of God being, did not esteem it something to be grasped to be equal with God. (Philippians 2:6)**

One must pay attention to the first part of the verse that says, "Who, in the form of God being." Literally, we could translate these words: "who *exists* in the form of God." It is important to emphasize that the verb "exists" is in the present tense, so that Shaul is telling us that Yeshua is always God. We see this also in the second part of the verse, where the same idea appears in other words: "Did not count equality with God a thing to be grasped." The literal translation is actually: "He did not think it was an *encroachment* to be equal to God." Clearly, through this verse, Shaul emphasized that even though Yeshua left heaven and donned flesh, He was not less than God.

✸ What sentence best describes Yeshua?

    a) Yeshua was born as a normal man and became God after He rose from the dead.

    b) Yeshua is always a combination of man and God.

    c) **Yeshua is the eternal son of God who came down from heaven and was incarnated.**

    d) Yeshua is the eternal son of God who came down from heaven and was incarnated, but was not really a person.

Now we are ready to learn about the Messiah's role.

The Messiah's Role

In Rambam's Mishneh Torah we find a list of things that the Messiah is expected to do. According to Judaism, from Rambam's days and on, until the Messiah will do all of those things, it is forbidden to declare someone as Messiah. It is important that all the acts that appear in Rambam's list have to do with what the Messiah will do in the End Times only, that is, at the end of the time period in which we currently live. Accordingly, until the Messiah comes (returns, according to our view) and finishes all of His work, it is forbidden to declare someone as the Messiah with certainty. Judaism today adopted this approach and follows it accordingly, though this rabbinic view is different from Yeshua's Jewish disciples. In his "Thirteen Principles" the Rambam wrote:

> I believe with perfect faith in the coming of the Messiah, and though He may tarry, still I await Him every day.

Rambam had faith in the coming of the Messiah, but as we have learned, this faith has to do with the recognition of the Messiah only after He finishes His work. Judaism focuses only on the Messiah's work at the end of days, while completely ignoring everything related to the Messiah's role of redeeming His people from sin. In addition, obvious signs are ignored regarding the Messiah's identity from a place of personal belief.

For example, Judaism does not accept the separation between God and mankind due to sin as the Prophet Isaiah says:

> Behold, not short is the hand of the LORD, from saving, and not dull is His ear from hearing; rather, your iniquities have made a separation between you and your God, and your sins have hidden (His) face from you from hearing. (Isaiah 59:1–2)

The redemption, according to Judaism, will come when all Israel will live according to the Torah, all their enemies will be defeated in the wars of God, they will worship God in the Third Temple, the outcasts of Israel will be ingathered and ascend to the Land of Israel, and in the end, the entire world will be repaired in order to serve God together as said:

> For then I will change to peoples a pure speech, to call, all of them in the name of the LORD to serve Him with one accord. (Zephaniah 3:9)

Although the Messiah will manifest all these things, before this He must save His people from sin. We believe that Yeshua from Nazareth redeemed us from sin forty years before the destruction of the Second Temple. Despite this, Judaism recognizes two Messiahs (Messiah son of Joseph and Messiah son of David). Judaism sees the work of Messiah son of Joseph as occurring only in the end of days, a short time before the coming of the Messiah son of David. According to Judaism, the purpose of the coming of Messiah son of Joseph is to call the people to repent and be prepared for the appearance of Messiah son of David. Accordingly, it is impossible to compare the idea of Messiah son of Joseph—according to Judaism—with the actions of Yeshua of Nazareth. Likewise, there is no significant meaning in Judaism today concerning the concept of Messiah son of Joseph.

✴ Judaism claims that it is forbidden to declare the identity of the Messiah until:

a) The Messiah brings all of Israel to walk in the ways of the Torah.

b) The Messiah wages the wars of the LORD.

c) The Messiah builds the Temple.

d) The Messiah will gather the outcasts of Israel.

e) **All of the above**

f) No correct answer

As disciples of Yeshua the Messiah, we do not accept the claim that there will be two messiahs, rather, that there is only One, Who will come twice, in order to fill two different roles. We can divide the first role into two parts: up until His death and after His death.

Until His Death

The first part begins with the incarnation as flesh and blood and ends with His crucifixion:

> **But Himself He emptied, a form of a servant taking, in the likeness of men being born. And (regarding) appearance, being found as of men, He humbled Himself, becoming obedient to the point of death, and death on a cross. (Philippians 2:7–8)**

In this paragraph we see the process through which Yeshua humbled Himself and emptied Himself in order to be a payment (redemption) for the sins of humanity. Yeshua's death did not only atone for the original sin (the sin of the Tree of Knowledge), but for all sin, iniquity, and transgression that mankind has done. The Messiah, as the mediator of salvation, reveals several important things about humanity's position in the presence of the Holy One: Since the primal sin, man is separated from God and in need of personal redemption; humanity cannot save itself. The cost of sin is written in the Torah of Moses:

> **And from the tree of the knowledge of good and evil you shall not eat from it, for in the day that you eat of it, you will surely die.** (Genesis 2:17)

The obvious question here is what is the meaning of the expression "you shall surely die"? Many people answer and say that this speaks of a physical death; however, the correct answer is a spiritual death. Of course, one of the results of spiritual death is also physical death. Death is the cost of sin that He charged every man to pay. The good news is that God gave us a solution to the heavy cost of death—which is that everyone who believes that Yeshua is the Messiah will be saved. At the same time, the fact that believers in Yeshua still die physically in this world attests to the fact that all the results of the Messiah's work have yet to be fully manifested.

Yeshua of Nazareth is the Messiah who redeems those who receive Him. He never sinned and therefore He can be the perfect sacrifice for us all. Readers of the New Covenant know that time and time again the leaders of Israel tried to prove that Yeshua had transgressed the commandments of the Torah, but they failed every time. The New Covenant reiterates that Yeshua was guiltless and followed the will of the Father perfectly. Only by merit of fulfilling all of these conditions can He grant eternal life to those who believe in Him.

Yeshua came to this world in order to give His life for sins. He spoke frequently about His expected death. Even though He is God, the goal of His first coming was not to be like God Almighty, as Yeshua also said:

> **For even the Son of Man did not come came to be served; rather but to serve, and to give His life as a ransom for many.** (Mark 10:45)

It can be said that from the moment of Yeshua's incarnation until His death almost everything that happened to Him had to do with His humiliation. This humiliation reveals to the reader how great Yeshua's love was for humanity and that He perfectly followed His Father, as it is written: **"He humbled Himself and submitted unto death, death on a cross."**

After Yeshua died on the cross, it is written that He went down to Sheol (hell):

> In saying, "He ascended," what is it if not but that He had also descended into the lower regions, the earth? (Ephesians 4:9)

Even though Yeshua died on the cross and went down to Sheol we read:

> Whom God raised, loosing the pangs of death, because it was not possible to hold Him by it. (Acts 2:24)

> Indeed our sickness He bore and our pains He suffered them and we considered stricken struck by God and afflicted. And He became rejected because of our transgression and because of our iniquities He was crushed, the punishment (for) our peace was upon Him and in His bruises we are healed. All of us like sheep have gone astray, a man his own way we has turned and hit Him with our iniquity. (Isaiah 53:4–6)

After His Death

The fact that death could not hold on to Yeshua reveals to the reader that Yeshua defeated death (sin). This verse shows and points out the meaningful transformation from Yeshua's humiliation to His glorification. Two events are connected with Yeshua's elevation: His resurrection and His ascension to heaven. It is important to remember two things regarding His resurrection: first, as we have learned, the fact that Yeshua rose from the dead proves that Yeshua defeated death (sin). We need to understand that there is a close connection between sin and death. The Apostle Shaul wrote "For the wages of sin is death, but the free gift of God is eternal life in Messiah Yeshua our Lord" (Romans 6:23). Even the Prophet Ezekiel stated "the sinning soul will die" (Ezekiel 18:20). It is important to note that Yeshua's resurrection did not reveal just His triumph over death, but testified that God the Father received Yeshua's service (sacrifice). In other words, the fact that the Holy One resurrected Yeshua (Acts 10:40, 13:30) proves that God found Yeshua's sacrifice worthy.

After Yeshua arose from the dead it is written that He appeared to many witnesses and on the fortieth day He ascended to heaven. What is the meaning of His ascent? Yeshua, in His physical form, emptied Himself and became a man. Yet even though Yeshua was fully man in every sense of the word, He did not cease for a moment to be divine in His essence. Yeshua did not become a man only in order to fulfill His destined role, but also to give humanity a perfect example of how each man needs to conduct himself and follow God's will. It is important to remember that when Yeshua ascended to heaven He actually returned to the place from which He descended. Yeshua is the Eternal Son of God, and therefore He *is* God.

Why did the Apostle Shaul write:

> **Therefore also God has highly exalted Him and freely placed on Him the name that is above every name, so that at the name of Yeshua every knee will bow, in heaven and on earth and under the earth, and every tongue will confess that Yeshua the Messiah is Lord, to the glory of God the Father. (Philippians 2:9–11)**

These verses do not describe a new status for Yeshua, but reveal His true identity to humanity. This subject can be divided into two parts: first, Yeshua is God. This is the meaning of the sentence **"and freely placed on Him the name that is above every name."** It is important to emphasize that Yeshua did not *become* God, rather, He always was God. Second, the merit of faith in Yeshua as Messiah, as it is written: **"so that at the name of Yeshua every knee will bow, in heaven and on earth and under the earth, and every tongue will confess that Messiah Yeshua is Lord, to the glory of God the Father."** Accordingly it can be understood why the Apostle Shimon (Peter) said:

> **And there is not in another, in no one is salvation, for not is there another name under heaven which is given among men, by which we must be saved. (Acts 4:12)**

CHAPTER 4

1) The epithet "Son of God" reveals that Yeshua of Nazareth is:
    a) Less than divine
    b) Has nothing to do with the divinity of the Messiah
    c) From the House of David
    d) Divine
    e) None of the above

2) It is written that all the families of the earth will see the Son of Man coming with the clouds of heaven. Despite the fact that the meaning of this verse is about the coming of the Messiah, its core meaning is:
    a) The time in which the Messiah will take all of His believers to heaven.
    b) The time in which the Messiah comes before God the Father in order to receive everything that comes to God.
    c) Only the coming of the Messiah at the end of days.
    d) A and C are correct.

3) Miriam (Mary) became pregnant with Yeshua by the Holy Spirit, but Yeshua did not become God until:
    a) He was immersed
    b) He finished His service and ascended to heaven
    c) This statement is incorrect since Yeshua was and always is God
    d) He rose from the dead

4) The Messiah is biologically descended from the House of David.
    a) True
    b) False

5) Yeshua of Nazareth rose to a divine level when it was said: **"and behold, a voice from heaven said, 'This is my beloved Son, with whom I am well pleased'"**?
    a) True
    b) False

6) If a Jew believes that God is one and that the Messiah will come, but does not accept Yeshua as the Messiah, is he saved?

    a) Yes, because all of the evil things that were done in the name of Christianity were done in Yeshua's name.

    b) No, because in spite of the evil things done in the name of Christianity, Jews still must believe in the name of Yeshua and that He is the Messiah.

7) In His Kingdom, the Messiah will lead the people of Israel to walk according to:

    a) God's Word

    b) The Torah of Moses

    c) The Holy Scriptures

    d) All of the above

    e) A and C

8) When Yeshua descended from heaven and emptied Himself, He:

    a) Lost His divinity

    b) Was no longer worthy to be worshiped

    c) Still God in His essence

9) People think that Yeshua died on the cross, but He really just faked it.

    a) True

    b) False

10) If Yeshua is God and yet died on the cross, did God die for three days?

    a) It is hard to believe, but this is the truth

    b) Only Yeshua's physical body died on the cross. It is, of course, impossible to kill God.

ANSWERS

1) D

2) B

3) C

4) False

5) False

6) B

7) D

8) C

9) B

10) B

THE HOLY SPIRIT

The term "Holy Spirit" (*Ruach HaKodesh*) does not appear on its own in the Hebrew Scriptures at all. Twice we find the expression "His Holy Spirit" (Isaiah 53:10–11), and once the combination "Your Holy Spirit" (Psalm 51:13). The term "Spirit of God" (*Ruach Elohim*) appears fifteen times, and similar expressions such as "*Ruach El*" and "*Ruach Eloha*" (also translated as "Spirit of God") can also be found referenced one time each. On the other hand, in the New Covenant we can find more than 250 direct references to the Holy Spirit. Although this chapter will deal mostly with the New Covenant's revelations about the Holy Spirit, the first part will discuss the conclusions that are reached in the Hebrew Bible regarding the Holy Spirit.

In Genesis, immediately after the creation of the world, it is written: **"And the Spirit of God hovers over the face of the waters."** What is the Spirit of God? Or more accurately, Who exactly is the Spirit of God? We must understand that the Spirit of God is not just a power but someone living, an entity:

> But they rebelled and grieved His Holy Spirit; therefore He turned to be their enemy, and He fought against them. (Isaiah 63:10)

The fact that the Holy Spirit can be grieved, teaches that He has feelings; in other words, it can be understood that He has a personality, and therefore we can have a relationship with Him. Yeshua taught on this subject when He said:

> If you love Me, My commandments you will keep. And I will ask the Father, and an Another Comforter, He will give to you, in order that He will remain with you forever, the Spirit of truth, Whom the world is not able to receive, because it neither sees Him nor knows Him. But you know Him, because with you He remains and in you He will be. I will not leave you (as) orphans; I will come to you. (John 14:15–18)

In this passage Yeshua taught His disciples that He would soon leave them and return to His Father in heaven. The separation between the disciples and their Rabbi is a very serious and important thing, and this is why Yeshua promised them that **"I will not leave you as orphans; I will come to you."** In this verse there seems to be a contradiction: on one hand, Yeshua said that He will leave His disciples, while on the other hand He promised that He would not leave them as orphans, alone. Accordingly, it makes sense to interpret this as Yeshua sending them a separate entity. When Yeshua continued and said, "I will come to you," He referred to the Holy Spirit. The fact that He said "*I* will come to you," even though He meant the Holy Spirit, reveals the close relationship between Yeshua and the Holy Spirit. In the verses that we have quoted, the relationship between Yeshua and the Holy Spirit can be seen, as well as the relationship between God the Father and the Holy Spirit, as it is written: **"I will ask the Father, and He will give you"** the Holy Spirit (the Comforter). In the same verse, regarding the Holy Spirit Yeshua said: **"(the Comforter will) be with you forever."** This sentence reveals to the reader that there is a great difference between what is said about the Holy Spirit in the New Covenant versus the Hebrew Scriptures.

✱ Is the relationship between the Holy Spirit and the believer temporary? Is it dependant solely upon the loyalty of the believer alone?

   a) Yes

   b) No

In the Scriptures, one of the tasks of the Holy Spirit is anointing. For example, it is written about David:

> **And Samuel took the horn of oil and he anointed him in the midst of his brothers. And the Spirit of the LORD came (rested) upon David from that day forward. And Samuel rose up and went to Ramah. (1 Samuel 16:13)**

We learn in the next verse that at the same time that David received the Holy Spirit, the Spirit left Saul: **"Now the Spirit of the LORD departed from Saul, and an evil spirit from the LORD tormented him"** (1 Samuel 16:14). In a different example, after David's sin with Bathsheba, David said: **"take not your Holy Spirit from me"** (Psalm 51:13). These examples point out that in the Scriptures the Holy Spirit could leave those who received Him. This fact makes it difficult to understand what Yeshua said about the Holy Spirit: **"(He will) be with you forever."** Why did Yeshua say that the Holy Spirit will be with the believer forever if there is proof from the Scriptures that He can leave someone who received His anointing? In the Scriptures the Holy Spirit descended upon certain people who were anointed for a certain position. By contrast, in the New Covenant people received the Holy Spirit through faith in Yeshua the Messiah. Through this faith, the believer enters an eternal covenant with the Holy One, which gives the believer eternal life—that is—the privilege to enter into the Kingdom of the LORD.

What does the Holy Spirit have to do with this promise? Shaul the Apostle answered in his epistle:

> He Who has worked (in) us for this same thing is God, the One Who has given to us the guarantee of the Spirit. Therefore being confident always and knowing that being at home in the body we are absent from the Lord. For by faith we walk not by sight, and we are confident and and we are pleased, rather to be away from the body and at home with the Lord. (2 Corinthians 5:5–8)

In these verses we read that the Holy Spirit is given as a "guarantee." What is the reason for this? In order to verify that the believer is truly saved. According to this principle, whoever has the Holy Spirit can be sure that if he dies, he will be separated from his physical body and will immediately be with the LORD.

Do you think that the Holy Spirit is in every believer? In Acts 19, we read that there were disciples that, despite being immersed in water, did not have the Holy Spirit:

> And it happened that while Apollos was in Corinth, Paul passed through the upper part to come to Ephesus. He found certain disciples (and) he said to them, "If the Holy Spirit you received after you believed?" And these said to him, "Not at all. If there is a Holy Spirit, we have not heard." (Acts 19:1–2)

It is important to pay attention to Shaul's (Paul) question: **"If you the Holy Spirit you received after you believed?"** This question could cause one to ponder: When someone comes to faith in Yeshua the Messiah, does the Holy One give him the Holy Spirit? From their response: **"Not at all. If there is a Holy Spirit, we have not heard."** it seems that they believed but had yet to receive the Holy Spirit. When Shaul heard their answer, he inquired:

> And he said to them, "Therefore into Whom were you baptized?" And these said to him, "Into the baptism of John." (Acts 19:3)

In spite of the fact that those people from Ephesus were called "disciples," they were not disciples of Yeshua the Messiah, rather only of Yochanan the Immerser (John the Baptist). They received Yochanan's message about repentance and the coming of the Messiah, but they never heard the name of Yeshua. Accordingly, Shaul continued and said:

> But Paul said, "John baptized a baptism of repentance; to the people (he was) saying, 'In the One who was coming after him, that they should believe, This is the One, in Messiah Yeshua." And after hearing, they were baptized in the name of the Lord Yeshua. And when Paul had laid his hands on them, the Holy Spirit came on them, and they were speaking in tongues and prophesying. (Acts 19: 4–6)

From here we see that these people were not really Yeshua's disciples until Shaul spoke the gospel to them and prayed with them, and so only after they had received Yeshua, the Holy Spirit came upon them immediately. There is an additional detail in these verses regarding the descent of the Holy Spirit: **"And when Paul had laid his hands on them, the Holy Spirit came on them."** Some say that the laying on of hands, in addition to faith in Yeshua, is necessary for receiving the Holy Spirit. Another place in Scripture that deals with this issue is also recorded in Acts:

> And after the apostles in Jerusalem heard that Samaria had received the word of God, they sent to them Peter and John, who came down and prayed for them so that they should receive the Holy Spirit, for as of yet, He had not yet fallen on any of them, but they had only been baptized in the name of the Lord Yeshua. Then they laid hands on them and they received the Holy Spirit. (Acts 8:14–17)

In chapter 19 the disciples were not disciples of Yeshua, while in chapter 8 we see that these are disciples of Yeshua the Messiah (they had only been baptized in the name of the Lord Yeshua). The fact that they believed in Yeshua and were immersed in His name, but had yet to receive the Holy Spirit, can strengthen the argument that the Holy Spirit can only be received by the laying on of hands, and not immediately when someone comes to faith in Yeshua. In Acts 10 we read:

> While Peter was still saying these words, the Holy Spirit fell on all who were hearing the word. And were amazed, the believers from among the circumcised, who had come with Peter, because also upon the Gentiles the gift of the Holy Spirit was poured out. For they were hearing them speaking in tongues and magnifying God. (Acts 10:44–46)

It appears that these two passages contradict one another. In chapter 10 they received the Holy Spirit and even spoke in tongues in spite of them never being immersed, and Shimon (Peter) did not lay his hands upon them. A case such as this, where one biblical text seems to contradict another, is nothing new. Rabbi Ishmael says: "The Torah is interpreted through thirteen principles." One of those principles fits this particular case: "When two texts seemingly contradict one another, a third text must come and determine between them." Throughout the New Covenant we find this principle repeating itself. When it comes to receiving the Holy Spirit. Shaul taught in his epistle to the Ephesians:

> In Whom also you, after you heard the word of truth, the Gospel of your salvation, in Whom also you believed (and) were sealed with the promised Holy Spirit, Who is the guarantee of our inheritance, for redemption of the purchased possession, for the praise of His glory. (Ephesians 1:13–14)

The Apostle Shaul taught that in addition to the fact that the Holy Spirit is given by faith, He is also a guarantee for those who believe in Yeshua the Messiah. Paul meant that each person who comes into covenant with the LORD through Yeshua is promised a place in the Kingdom of God. If so, since we have learned that faith is enough to save and to receive the Holy Spirit, how can we explain the event in Acts chapter 8? It is important to understand that this passage from Acts chapter 8 is about the first time that Samaria received the gospel. The herald of the gospel to the Samaritans was Philip, who is named in Acts chapter 6, but not as one of the emissaries. The fact that it is clearly written: **"And after the apostles heard in Jerusalem that Samaria received the word of God, they sent to them Peter and John"** is very important. The purpose of this story is in verse 15: "[they] came down and prayed for them that they should receive the Holy Spirit." The question arises: How could the emissaries know that the Samaritans had yet to receive the Holy Spirit? The answer is found in Yeshua's words that He said before ascending to heaven:

> **But You will receive power when the Holy Spirit has come upon you, and you will be my witnesses in Jerusalem and in all Judea and Samaria, and to the end of the earth. (Acts 1:8)**

This verse means that the receiving of the Holy Spirit *at first* only occurred through the Apostles. This can be understood from the verse: **"The Spirit was given through the laying on of the Apostles' hands."** It is important to understand that the main interest in these verses from chapter 8 is the authority of the Apostles and not the way one receives the Holy Spirit. As we have said, **in the beginning**, the receiving of the Holy Spirit was in the laying on of the Apostles' hands, and this was in order to strengthen their authority, but obviously the Apostles would not be around permanently. After the Holy Spirit spread throughout Jerusalem, Judea, Samaria, and even outside of the Holy Land, true faith in Yeshua the Messiah is always accompanied with the receiving of Holy Spirit. That is, anyone who believes in Yeshua has the ability to discover the gifts of the Spirit and to have intimacy with God from the moment that he comes to faith.

✸ In addition to faith, in order to receive that Holy Spirit a believer must:

   a) Be baptized in Yeshua's name

   b) Have another believer with the Holy Spirit lay his hands upon him

   c) A and B are correct

   d) None of the above

The Work of the Holy Spirit

The Holy Spirit acts in various ways. Generally, it can be said that the Spirit equips the believer in all the necessary tools in order to serve God. When Yeshua taught about the Holy Spirit He said that the Spirit will console the believer and guide him to all truth. An additional role of the Holy Spirit is to convict the world of its sin, to bring justice, and to give judgment. In other words, He teaches the believers everything and reminds them of everything that Yeshua said.

✸ The Holy Spirit has various and different roles, they are:

   a) Consoling the believer

   b) Teaching the believer

   c) Equipping the believer

   d) Helping the believer

   e) Instructing the believer

   f) All of the above

From the Holy Scripture it is clear that the Holy Spirit dwells in every believer and gives him strength, so much so that Yeshua said:

> Truly, truly, I say to you, the one who believes in Me, the works which I do, that one will do; and greater works than these, will he do, because I, to the Father go. (John 14:12)

An additional role of the Spirit is to help believers in prayer. It was told to us that believers *must* pray in the Spirit: **"Praying at all times in the Spirit, with all prayer and supplication"** (Ephesians 6:18).

Likewise, there are times when we do not know what to pray for or how to pray, and in times like these Shaul taught:

> And likewise the Spirit helps us in our weakness. For what we should pray, according to what is necessary, we do not know, but He, the Spirit intercedes for us with groanings too deep for words. And He Who searches hearts knows what is the mind of the Spirit, because He according to God intercedes on behalf of saints. (Romans 8:26–27)

The Holy Spirit is connected with the sanctification of the believer. That is to say, every believer is meant to mature through the Spirit, by means of the renewing of the mind, in order to reflect Yeshua's image in thought and action. Many times Yeshua told His disciples not to walk in accordance with the flesh (the evil inclination, *yetzer hara*), but by the Spirit. Only through the Holy Spirit can Shaul's instruction be followed: **"Take every thought captive to obey Messiah"** (2 Corinthians 10:5). There is a close connection between sanctification and God's will. In other words, only when the believer acts and behaves according to God's plans, he advances in holiness, and the Holy One acts in his life and unifies him with the image of the Son of God. In this manner the Holy Spirit will reward the believer with attributes called "the fruit of the Spirit."

> And the fruit of the Spirit is love, joy, peace, patience, kindness, goodness, faithfulness, gentleness, self-control; against such things there is no law. (Galatians 5:22–23)

In addition to this fruit, the Spirit also gives believers gifts. These gifts prepare believers to serve Yeshua and continue His work. Two main places in the New Covenant speak about spiritual gifts. The first is in Romans:

> For just as in one body we have many parts, and the parts do not all have the same function, Thus, we are many (in) one body, in Messiah, and individually parts of one another. And having different gifts according to the grace having been given to us. If prophecy, according to the proportion to the faith; if ministry, in the ministry; if one teaches, in the teaching; if one exhorts, in the exhortation; the one who gives, in generosity; the one who leads, in zeal; the one who is merciful, in cheerfulness. (Romans 12:4–8)

From this passage, seven gifts can be discerned:

a) Prophecy

b) Service

c) Teaching

d) Encouragement and rebuking

e) Generosity

f) Leadership

g) Mercy

The second place where we read about the gifts of the Spirit is in the first epistle to the Corinthians:

> And there are varieties of gifts, but the same Spirit. And there are varieties of ministries, and the same Lord; and there are varieties of workings, but it is the same God the One Who empowers all in all. For to each one is given the manifestation of the Spirit for the common good. For to one through the Spirit is given a word of wisdom, and to another a word of knowledge according to the same Spirit, to another faith in the same Spirit, to another gifts of healing in the same Spirit, to another the working of miracles, to another prophecy, to another the ability to distinguish spirits, and to another various kinds of tongues, and to another the interpretation of tongues. But all these are empowered in One

> **and the same Spirit, Who distributes personally just as He wills.**
> (1 Corinthians 12:4–11)

In this passage nine gifts appear:

a) Wisdom

b) Knowledge

c) Faith

d) Healing

e) Miracle Working

f) Prophecy

g) Discerning between spirits

h) Tongues

i) Interpretation of tongues

Our goal in this book is not to teach or explain the meaning of each of these gifts, but it is good to clear up a few points:

- The Holy Spirit distributes the spiritual gifts to every believer (**"The same Spirit, Who distributes personally just as He wills"**).

- Only when believers collectively work together, and each believer uses his gift within the community, will the community receive the best result from the Holy Spirit. In this context, Shaul likened the community of Messiah to a building:

> **In Whom all the building, being joined together, grows into a Holy Sanctuary in the Lord. In Whom you also are being built together into a dwelling place of God in (the) Spirit. (Ephesians 2:21–22)**

- Every believer has at least one gift, but there is no one man who has all of the gifts of the Spirit.

- There is no special gift that all believers have that could be considered as proof that a believer truly received the Holy Spirit.

CHAPTER 5

1) Is there a difference between the **works** of the Holy Spirit in the Hebrew Scriptures and in the New Covenant?

   a) No, the Holy Spirit functions in the exact same way.

   b) Yes, in the Hebrew Scriptures the Holy Spirit anointed a person to a position, while in the New Covenant it acts in many other ways.

   c) None of the above

2) Regarding our salvation, Shaul called the Holy Spirit:

   a) The consoler

   b) The spirit of truth

   c) The intercessor

   d) The guarantee

3) Yeshua told the disciples: **"You will receive power when the Holy Spirit has come upon you, and you will be My witnesses in Jerusalem and in all Judea and Samaria, and to the end of the earth."** This verse reveals to the reader that the Holy Spirit is given to believers by the Apostles upon their first arrival in Judea, Samaria, and the Diaspora. This fact refers to:

   a) The Apostle's authority.

   b) Only special believers receive the Holy Spirit.

   c) None of the above

4) Prayer is a very important matter. The Holy Spirit helps the believer to know how to pray and what to pray for.

   a) True

   b) False

5) The first step in faith is salvation, and afterwards each believer must continue on the path of sanctification. Is there a connection between the Holy Spirit and the believer's process of sanctification?

   a) Yes

   b) No

6) What attribute is not one of the fruits of the Spirit?

   a) Love

   b) Joy

   c) Patience

   d) Generosity

   e) Complaints

   f) Mercy

   g) Faith

7) Are the fruits of the Spirit opposed to the character of the Torah?

   a) Yes

   b) No

8) The main reason that the Holy Spirit gives a believer gifts is:

   a) In order for the believer to serve Yeshua within the community.

   b) In order for those who received more unique gifts to be more important.

   c) In order for believers to honor God.

   d) A + C

9) There is one certain gift that all believers have.

   a) True

   b) False

10) There is a way to choose which gift of the Holy Spirit a believer will receive.

   a) True

   b) False

ANSWERS

1) B

2) D

3) A

4) True

5) Yes

6) E

7) No

8) D

9) False

10) False

THE COMMUNITY OF THE MESSIAH AND DISCIPLESHIP

In the New Covenant, there is a Greek word that describes the Messiah's community. This word is ἐκκλησία (*ekklesia*). This word is actually a combination of two words: the first is *ek*, which means "out", and the second is *klesia*, which means "to call." The word *ekklesia* appears in the Septuagint (Greek translation of the Torah) in the Book of Exodus, and there it is used to describe the people who came out of Egypt by means of the Passover offering. It is important to note that every person who was redeemed from Egypt took part in the Passover sacrifice, and there is no disagreement between interpreters that the blood is the key part of the various sacrifices. Therefore it is clear to all that without the blood of the Passover lamb, no man could have gone from bondage to freedom. It is not by chance that Yeshua was crucified on Passover, and Shaul called Yeshua our Passover lamb: **"For also our Passover lamb, on behalf of us, has been sacrificed—Messiah"** (1 Corinthians 5:7). We need to understand that the exodus from Egypt represents our faith in Messiah Yeshua. Likewise, it is quite an interesting parallel that the name given to the community that went out of Egypt—*ekklesia* in the Septuagint—was also the name given to those who received the Gospel of Messiah in the New Covenant. According to the New Covenant, to be a member of the Messiah's community there is a need to believe in the gospel of Messiah Yeshua. Yeshua once asked His disciples: **"But who do you say that I am?"** (Matthew 16:15). **"Simon Peter replied, 'You are the Messiah, the Son of the living God'"** (Matthew 16:16). It is interesting to notice that immediately after Shimon (Simon Peter) identified Yeshua as Messiah, Yeshua began speaking about the *Ekklesia*:

> And Yeshua answered (and) said to him, "Blessed are you, Simon Bar-Jonah! because flesh and blood did not reveal this to you, but My Father Who is in the heavens. And I say to you, that you are Peter, and upon this rock I will build My Church and the gates of

> **hell will not be stronger than it. And I will give to you the keys of the Kingdom of Heaven."** (Matthew 16:17–19a)

In these verses, Yeshua added a name to Shimon and called him "Peter" (Petros). The meaning of the word *petros* means "rock," and in various places in the New Covenant the name Peter is used interchangeably with the Aramaic name "Keifa [Cephas]" ("rock" in Aramaic). In the English translation, verse 18 says, **"and on this rock I will build My church** (community/*ekklesia*)." Even though the Hebrew translator chose to use another word for rock here (*tzur*), there are those who claim that the word אבן, *even* (literally, "stone") is more suitable to Yeshua' play on words—"and on this Rock I will build My community."

What was Yeshua's intent in choosing the word "rock"? The answer is in Shimon Keifa's (Peter's) answer regarding Yeshua's identity: **"You are the Messiah, the Son of the living God."** In other words, only when someone identifies Yeshua of Nazareth as the Messiah, Son of God, he becomes part of His community (*ekklesia*).

The connection between Yeshua and the *ekklesia* is so close that the New Covenant even describes the community of believers as the body of Messiah:

> **Towards the perfecting of the saints for the work of ministry, for building up the body of Messiah.** (Ephesians 4:12)

This verse mentions the role of the Messianic community as a "work of ministry," meaning that the Messianic community is meant to serve the Holy One.

Community Service

According to the definition in the Holy Scriptures, the community of Messiah is built up of people rather than bricks, despite the fact that in the previous verse in Ephesians the word "building" appears. The Apostle Shaul chose to use this word for two reasons: first, that the Messianic community be built up (grow) through service. Shaul meant that the Messianic community would be strengthened only as long as it serves the will of God. The second reason is that the Messianic community can only serve when the Holy Spirit dwells within it. The use of the term "building" is symbolic and meant to hint toward the Sanctuary (the unique dwelling place of God). In the past, the Holy Spirit dwelled within the Sanctuary, in the building that was built by people, physically, but now the Holy Spirit dwells in those who belong to the body of Messiah.

The Messianic community has four main purposes:

a) Worshiping God

b) Personal growth/ strengthening

c) Missions

d) General service

Serving God and the Messianic community: only believers in Yeshua can serve God as He wants His devoted followers to serve Him now. As it is written:

> But an hour is coming, and now is, when the true worshipers will worship the Father in spirit and truth, for also the Father is seeking such people to worship Him. God is Spirit, and the ones who worship Him in Spirit and truth it is necessary to worship. (John 4:23–24)

Only believers in Messiah Yeshua have the ability and privilege to worship God in Spirit and truth, since the Holy Spirit dwells only within Yeshua's followers.

The Apostle Shaul emphasized that in whichever place the worship of God takes place, **"All things decently and in order shall be done"** (1 Corinthians 14:40). Additionally, we see that there are different types of divine service:

> Therefore what then, brothers? When you come together, each of you a hymn have, a teaching have, a tongue have, a revelation have, an interpretation have. All things to build up, shall be done. (1 Corinthians 14:26)

The service of God is not limited to one day; it must be done every day of the week. Daniel prayed to God three times every day: **"Daniel ... went to his house where he had windows in his upper chamber open toward Jerusalem. He got down on his knees three times a day and prayed and gave thanks before his God."** (Daniel 6:11)

There are Christian theologians who claimed in the past, and even still claim today, that since Yeshua rose from the dead, the Sabbath changed from Saturday to Sunday. One of the passages that they quote in order to support their argument is:

> And concerning the collection for the saints: just as I directed the churches of Galatia, so you also are to do. Each first day of week, let each of you from himself, put something aside and store it

> up, in order that he may prosper, in order that whenever I come
> there will be no collecting. (1 Corinthians 16:1–2)

These verses have nothing to do with formal worship services. Most Christian theologians concluded that since donations are collected during their meetings, and Shaul referred to this day as the first day (Sunday), the first believers thereby also met on Sundays. This interpretation is wrong since we must remember that in days of old, most people received their wages at the end of each work day. Shaul teaches us here that donations to God should not be given from the left overs of the wages at the end of the week, but they should be given at the beginning. This lesson is very similar to the commandment to give a tithe, which is also given from the first of the produce, as it is written:

> And it shall come about when you enter into the land which the
> LORD your God gives to you, an inheritance, and you shall pos-
> sess it and dwell in it. And you shall take from the first of all the
> fruit of the land which you shall bring from your land which the
> LORD your God gives to you and you shall set it in a basket and
> you shall go to the place where the LORD your God will choose
> for His name to dwell there. (Deuteronomy 26:1–2)

Let us emphasize that, just as we learned, each day is suitable for the worship of God, and it would be a mistake to attribute the worship of God only to the Sabbath day.

Personal growth/strengthening: in the same way that we were born as babies in the flesh, so too, we are described as newborn babies after we were reborn in the Spirit. All of us, when we were born, were babies and slowly learned to crawl, sit, speak, stand, and walk. Every believer has the responsibility to strengthen and mature in faith through personal growth following Yeshua's example. As the body of Messiah we can strengthen ourselves only when every believer acts in the framework of the gifts of the Spirit he was given. In this way, not only will each one of us contribute to the body of Messiah as a whole, but we will also help each other to personally grow and strengthen, and in so doing we will be able to put Shaul's instruction into action, which says that every believer must use his gifts and abilities to help other believers grow and strengthen in Messiah:

> That there may be no division in the body, but the same, in be-
> half of one another, they care for (all) parts. And if one suffers,

> all parts suffer together; if one part is honored, all parts rejoice
> together. And you are the body of Messiah and individually parts
> of it. (1 Corinthians 12:25-27)

The challenge of all believers is to be **"rooted and built up in Him (Yeshua) and
having been established in the faith, just as you were taught, abounding in it in
thanksgiving"** (Colossians 2:7). In other words, believers are described in Scripture
as children who need to grow in faith and change from children into adults (in understanding and in deed). The author of the epistle to the Hebrews described this
as follows:

> For everyone who partakes of milk is unskilled of the word
> of righteousness, for a child is he. But he is mature, (if) the
> solid food, he is constantly using (this one has developed) the
> senses (and) has been trained for discerning both good and evil.
> (Hebrews 5:13-14)

Only someone strong in faith can "discern both good and evil," that is, to discern
between God's will and sin. It is not enough to know these things, but to also implement them in practice.

Commission: the commission of every disciple of Messiah Yeshua is to represent
Him (to be an ambassador) in the world and to make new disciples. The first thing
that Yeshua told His disciples was:

> And Yeshua came He spoke to them, saying "It has been given
> to Me all authority in heaven and upon earth. Therefore go and
> teach all nations baptizing them in the name of the Father and of
> the Son and of the Holy Spirit; teaching them to keep all which
> I have commanded you. And behold, I am with you all the days,
> until the end of the age." (Matthew 28:18-20)

> Therefore, on behalf of Messiah, we are ambassadors, as God
> making His exhorting through us. We implore on behalf of Mes-
> siah, be reconciled to God. (2 Corinthians 5:20)

Each of Messiah Yeshua's devoted followers is called to the mission of making more
disciples. It is clear from these verses that Yeshua gave this authority to His disciples

so that every believer would be able to use it and make disciples. This process is made up of three tasks that we must fulfill:

a) Making new disciples (spreading the Gospel)

b) Immersing new believers

c) Teaching believers about keeping Yeshua's commandments

These three tasks are of equal importance and they are connected to each other. Spreading the gospel is important in order for there to be new disciples, immersing is important as a testimony and declaration of the faith, and teaching the keeping of Yeshua's commandments is important as a testimony that we belong to Him.

This mission is similar to what is written in the book of Proverbs, **"Whoever takes souls is wise"** (11:30). The word "take" alludes to fact that the wise person takes people, meaning that He *brings* them to personal salvation by means of the gospel. Beyond this, this verse in its entirety is quite interesting:

> **Righteous fruit is a tree of life, and the one who takes souls is wise. (Proverbs 11:30)**

In the first half of the verse there are two important word combinations: "the fruit of the righteous" and "tree of life". "Righteous fruit" refers to the good acts of the Righteous One, Messiah Yeshua, who gave his life on the cross (also called "tree")— "tree of life." From this verse we can determine that Yeshua did God's work, the redemption, when He died upon the tree, and as a result of this, any act to bring others to believe in Yeshua will be considered righteous.

Yeshua gave His disciples an additional command concerning immersion, which we will learn about more in the rest of the chapter. We will just say now that immersion is connected with a believer's responsibility to Yeshua in faith and in action.

General service: this matter can be summed up in one sentence: **"You will love your neighbor as yourself."** There are two aspects to upholding this commandment: the first physical, as it is written about the first believers:

> **And all who believed were together and had all things in common. And possessions and goods they were selling and dividing them to all, as anyone had need. (Acts 2:44–45)**

The second relates to the spiritual state of the believer, and this is what the Apostle Shaul taught:

> Brothers, if also a man is caught in any transgression, you the ones who are spiritual, restore such a person in a spirit of gentleness. Considering yourself, lest you also be tempted. Bear one another's burdens, and thus you will fulfill the Torah of the Messiah. (Galatians 6:1–2)

These two aspects encompass one idea which Shaul articulates in his epistle to the Philippians:

> Fulfill my joy, in order that you are of the same mind, having the same love, united in soul thinking the same. Nothing according to self desire or according to vain conceit, but in the humility, one another esteeming beyond themselves, Not the things belonging to themselves, each should be considering, but the things of each others'. Have this mind be you, which also (was) in Messiah Yeshua. (Philippians 2:2–5)

In conclusion, we must understand that as disciples of Messiah Yeshua, it is our duty to care for others, both spiritually and physically.

Immersion

Many people think that the commandment of immersion is based on Yochanan the Immerser (John the Baptist), but the truth is that this is an ancient Jewish tradition. Archeological discoveries and other sources show that people kept this tradition at least from the First Temple Period, and perhaps even earlier. There are several interpretations regarding the meaning of immersion.

In Judaism, generally, the purpose of immersion is to change the status of a person or a vessel from impure to pure. For example, a priest cannot serve God until he has immersed, meaning that the immersion is preparation for service.

Despite the fact that Yochanan did not institute the practice of immersion, it can be said that he gave it an additional meaning. Yochanan's immersion was of repentance, as it is written:

> John came, baptizing in the desert and proclaiming a baptism of repentance for the forgiveness of sins. (Mark 1:4)

> And Shaul said, "John baptized with the baptism of repentance, to the people saying, for One is coming after him in order that they should believe, this is, in Messiah Yeshua. (Acts 19:4)

We can see that this immersion is different in two aspects: The first is the desire to turn away from sin (repentance), and the second is the desire to follow God's plans. Therefore, when one of Yeshua's disciples is immersed, it is important that he admit his sins and express readiness to do God's will.

While Yochanan was immersing people in the desert we are told that:

> Then Yeshua came from the Galilee to the Jordan to John, to be baptized by him. But John forbade Him, saying, "I have need by You to be baptized and you come to Me?" But Yeshua answered him (and) said, "Let it be now, for thus it is to us to fulfill all righteousness." Then he allowed Him. (Matthew 3:13–15)

Why did Yeshua come to be immersed by Yochanan? As we have learned, the immersion represents a change in a person's status and also a preparation for service. This is confirmed in that immediately after His immersion, Yeshua began His service on earth. It is important to emphasize that Yeshua's immersion was only to affirm what was said, for it is clear that Yeshua never sinned, so He had no need to repent. Therefore, Yeshua's immersion was connected to the second aspect that we spoke of, that is, the desire to obey the plans of His Father in heaven. Likewise, we must understand that there is a close connection to God's will when it comes to Yeshua and to immersion. In other words, the immersion symbolizes Yeshua's ministry, and due to this, Yeshua Himself described His death on the cross, His burial, and His resurrection as an immersion.

> But I have a baptism to be baptized and how I am distressed, until it will be completed! (Luke 12:50)

Yeshua said this after being immersed in the Jordan, therefore He was not referring to His immersion in water; rather, to what would happen to Him in Jerusalem. This verse can be used as proof that His death, burial, and resurrection can be called an immersion. Also, after Yeshua was immersed by Yochanan we read:

> And when Yeshua was baptized, He went up immediately from the water, and behold, the heavens were opened to Him, and He

> saw the Spirit of God coming down as a dove and coming on Him; and behold, a voice from the heavens saying, "This is My Beloved Son, in Whom I am well pleased." (Matthew 3:16–17)

What is the meaning of the voice that was heard, saying **'This is My Beloved Son, in Whom I am well pleased."**? Yeshua's immersion was a sign to His Father that Yeshua intended to accomplish God's plan of redemption by dying on the cross, being buried, and being resurrected on the third day. This interpretation can be found in Peter's words in one of his epistles:

> For also Messiah, once for sins suffered (died), the Righteous One on behalf of the unrighteous ones, in order that He might bring us to God, being put to death in the flesh, but made alive in the Spirit, which also to the ones in prison—spirits (the souls of the dead); He went, He proclaimed, they who, because they formerly did not obey, when God's patience waited in the days of Noah, while the ark was being prepared, in which a few, that is, eight souls (people), were saved through water. Baptism, which also is now a typology of this, saves , not as a removal of dirt from the flesh, but a request to God of a good conscience, by means of the resurrection of Messiah Yeshua. (1 Peter 3:18–21)

In other versions, the word "died" in the first verse of this passage appear as "suffered." It is interesting to know that in the original language the verb is πάσχω (*pascho*), a Greek root whose origin comes from the Hebrew פסח (*pesach*). It is reasonable to assume that the version that was quoted above is newer and the translator chose the easier word that is more easily understood for those who do not have a Jewish background. In other words, in the first translations the word "suffered" (made our Passover lamb) was used, but later on, they used the verb "to die" to explain Messiah's suffering. In every sense, the verse's meaning is that Yeshua died on the cross (and He did so on Passover).

While the main subject in verse 18 is Yeshua's death, the fact that afterward Yeshua "went and proclaimed to the spirits (people) in prison" reveals that Yeshua went down to Sheol (Hell), and likewise verse 19 speaks of Yeshua's burial. In verse 21 immersion is mentioned: **"Baptism, which also is now a typology of this, saves."** Does the verse mean that immersion saves people? Most certainly not! Because it then says: **"not as a removal of dirt from the flesh, but a request to God of a good conscience, by means of the resurrection of Messiah Yeshua."** It is important to note that the end of the verse speaks about Yeshua's resurrection. If so, what is the meaning of this verse? To teach the reader that immersion in water by itself does not save, but rather what saves is what it represents! That is, the real immersion—Yeshua's death, burial, and resurrection. Therefore, when someone believes in Yeshua's work, death, burial, and resurrection, he is saved. There are four main points regarding immersion that every disciple of Yeshua needs to affirm and admit before he is immersed:

a) General repentance—a personal desire to turn away from sin and return to God, including confession of personal sins.

b) Personal repentance—the desire to follow God's will regarding His personal plan for every person.

c) Identification with Yeshua's death, burial, and resurrection as the only way to be saved.

d) The immersion in water represents the work of Yeshua, which saves the believer.

According to Scripture, the immersion must be a complete immersion and is only performed after one has affirmed these four points.

Communion

An additional command that Yeshua gave the body of Messiah is communion. Similar to immersion, the Last Supper symbolizes Yeshua's service for salvation. Since communion is connected with redemption, it is not surprising that Yeshua declared this command during Passover during His Last Supper. Communion is also known as "the Lord's Supper," though this "supper" is made up of two things: matzah (unleavened bread) and wine. In the New Covenant we read about this commandment:

> **And He took bread, and after He gave thanks, He broke (it) and gave it to them, saying, "This is My body, which in behalf of you it is given. This you do in remembrance of Me." Likewise also the cup after the eating, saying, "This cup is the New Covenant in My blood, which on behalf of you is poured out." (Luke 22:19–20)**

Yeshua used unleavened bread (Matza) to teach His disciples what He was about to do in the next few hours—giving up His life (His body) as the Passover offering. In the Scriptures the term לחם (*lechem*) is generally translated as bread, but in ancient Hebrew it more symbolically represents daily food we need to live. This is the reason Yeshua said in His prayer: **"Give us today our daily bread."** Even though in the verses that we have quoted from Luke's Gospel the word "bread" appears, it is important to understand that Yeshua used matza because there is a special significance in unleavened bread. The Apostle Shaul spoke about the special property of matza in his epistle to the Corinthians:

> Not good your boasting. Do you not know that a little leaven, the whole lump leavens? Therefore, cleanse out the old leaven in order that you may be a new lump, just as you are unleavened. For also Messiah, our Passover lamb, in our behalf has been sacrificed. So that we therefore will keep the festival, not with the old leaven, the leaven of malice and evil, but with the unleavened bread of sincerity and truth. (1 Corinthians 5:6–8)

Later, Yeshua likened the wine to His blood, saying that the blood was connected to the New Covenant. Here we have another example of how Yeshua associated almost everything He taught and did to the Hebrew Scriptures. The Prophet Jeremiah prophesied about the New Covenant, saying:

> Behold the days are coming, declares the LORD, and I will cut with the house of Israel and with the house of Judah a New Covenant. Not as the covenant which I cut with their fathers in the day I took them by the hand to bring them out from the land of Egypt, which they broke My covenant, and I was a husband to them, declares the LORD. For this is the covenant which I will cut with the house of Israel after those days, declares the LORD I place My Torah in their midst and upon their heart I wrote it and I will be to them God and they shall be to Me for a people. A man will not teach anymore his friend nor a man his brother saying, 'Know the LORD', for all of them shall know Me, from the least of them unto the greatest of them, declares the LORD because I will forgive their iniquity and their sins I will remember no more. (Jeremiah 31:31–34)

In this covenant there are two new ideas: First, the Holy One will put His Torah within us and write it on our hearts. Second, He will forgive our iniquity and remember our sin no more. As the prophet reveals to the reader these two matters, there appears a sentence which frequently is found in Scripture: "And I will be their God, and they shall be my people," According to the sages, this sentence is the fundamental definition of the redemption. In that meal, as we have read, that Yeshua took the cup after they had eaten and said, **"This cup is the New Covenant in My blood, which on behalf of you is poured out."** According to tradition, the cup after the meal is called the Cup of Redemption. Shaul taught about this commandment as well:

> For I received from the Lord which also I have delivered to you, that the Lord Yeshua on the night which He was betrayed took bread, and after He gave thanks, He broke it, and said, "Take, eat, This is My body, which in behalf of you is broken. This do in remembrance of Me." Likewise also the cup after the dining saying, "This cup is the new covenant in My blood. This do, whenever you drink (it is) for My remembrance. For whenever you eat this bread and this cup you drink, the death of the Lord you proclaim now until He should come. So that whomever eats this bread or drinks the cup of the Lord unworthily will be guilty of the body and blood of the Lord and let a man examine himself and thusly from the bread let him eat and from the cup let him drink. For the one who eats and drinks unworthily, judgment upon himself he eats and drinks, not discerning the body of the Lord. On account of this, many among you are weak and sick and many have fallen asleep. But if ourselves we judge, then we will not be judged. But being judged by the Lord we are disciplined in order than not with the world we should be condemned. So then my brothers, when coming together to eat, wait for one another and if a certain one is hungry, at home let him eat; in order not for judgment you have come together and the remaining things, when I should come, I will set in order. (1 Corinthians 11:23–34)

Shaul understood that Yeshua's work on the cross, which communion symbolizes, is connected to the New Covenant. We learn from Shaul that the goal of this commandment is to remind people of Yeshua's death on the cross (the redemption of sinners) until He returns. Due to the importance of this commandment and the meaning that accompanies it, Shaul warned people (believers only!) to take the bread and wine in a worthy manner, not to take it lightly, but rather with the right intention and seriousness. Shaul said: "Let a person examine himself, then so eat of the bread and drink of the cup," meaning that each and every believer needs to do some soul-searching before he takes part in the Lord's Supper. If someone takes the communion inappropriately, God forbid, this can have dire consequences, as it is written: **"That is why many of you are weak and ill, and some have died (fallen asleep)."**

In conclusion, the immersion and the communion are two very special and meaningful matters for the Messianic community and, accordingly, every believer should learn these commandments and rules.

CHAPTER 6

1) Every person who was redeemed from Egypt had:

   a) A heart ready to serve God

   b) Many good deeds

   c) Faith in Moses

   d) The Passover experience

2) What is the central motif in any sort of sacrifice?

   a) Prayer

   b) Blood

   c) Suffering

   d) Fasting

3) The exodus from Egypt represents:

   a) Faith in Messiah Yeshua

   b) The result of observing the commandments

   c) The strength of the people of Israel

   d) None of the above

4) In order to be part of the Messianic community, each person must:

   a) Be Jewish

   b) Believe in the authority of the Torah alone

   c) Be righteous

   d) Believe that Yeshua is the Passover sacrifice

5) The Messianic community is called:

   a) To serve God

   b) To only learn Talmud

   c) To materialistically succeed in this world

   d) To receive respect and love from the public

6) The Messianic community can serve God only when it:

   a) Obeys God's will

   b) Serves with the help of the anointing of the Holy Spirit

   c) All of the above

   d) None of the above

7) Every person can serve God in his current state.

   a) True

   b) False

8) How many days in the week are intended for service of God? _____

9) Daniel worshiped God _____ times every day.

10) Since Yeshua was resurrected on Sunday, the Sabbath was changed from Saturday to Sunday.

   a) True

   b) False

11) In order to serve God, every believer must use:

   a) His physical strength

   b) His intellect

   c) His feelings

   d) The gifts of the Spirit

12) It is not enough to just know God's will, we must also _____ this knowledge in our lives!

13) Every believer must spread the message of our faith.

   a) Yes

   b) No

14) A disciple of Yeshua must:

   a) Make more disciples

   b) Encourage people who have received the good news to be immersed in Yeshua's name

   c) Teach believers to keep Yeshua's commandments

   d) All of the above

15) Yeshua's death, burial, and resurrection were likened to _____.

16) A person coming to be immersed needs to:

    a) Recognize that he is a sinner

    b) Declare his will to abandon sin and obey Yeshua

    c) Receive in faith Yeshua's death as atonement for all his sins

    d) Believe that Yeshua was resurrected

    e) All of the above

17) Communion has to do with the New _____.

18) In communion, the matza represents Yeshua's _____ and the wine His _____.

19) Anyone can take part in communion, even if he does not believe in Yeshua yet.

    a) True

    b) False

20 Despite someone taking communion inappropriately, there will not be physical consequences.

    a) True

    b) False

1) D

2) B

3) A

4) D

5) A

6) C

7) False

8) 7

9) 3

10) False

11) D

12) Apply

13) Yes

14) D

15) Immersion

16) E

17) Covenant

18) Body, blood

19) False

20 False

TORAH AND SALVATION

The word "salvation" can be interpreted as unity between man and God. The first question that we shall examine in this chapter is: Does the Torah have a role in saving people? In order to understand the purpose of the Torah regarding this question, we must first understand the meaning of the covenant that God made with our father, Abraham. Shaul wrote regarding this:

> **And to Abraham the promises were made and to His Seed. It does not say, "And to seeds," as to many, but as to One, "And to your Seed," who is Messiah. And this is I say (the) Covenant being confirmed beforehand by God in Messiah, the one having come 430 years afterward—the Torah (Law), does not annul as to nullify the promise. (Galatians 3:16–17)**

In these verses, we find two important points: first, there is a connection between Abraham's covenant and Messiah, the Redeemer of Israel. Second, the Torah cannot cancel or break a covenant that was made 430 years prior. It is important to emphasize that the covenant with Abraham was not intended **only** for Abraham or for the Jews, but for all of humanity, as it is written: **"And will be blessed in you, *all* the families of the earth."** (Genesis 12:3). Abraham's covenant and the Torah have something in common: righteousness. The Torah defines what it means to be righteous, while Abraham's covenant shows the path to it. How can a person find righteousness according to Abraham's covenant? The answer is found in Genesis: **"And [Abraham] believed in the LORD, and He accounted it for him righteousness"** (Genesis 15:6). This verse teaches the reader that righteousness, in God's eyes, depends on faith and is not based on good deeds (observance of the commandments). If so, why was the Torah given? The reason is that the people of Israel did not live according to the faith of their forefathers, therefore God gave Moses the Torah in order to reveal to the children of Israel how far they were from God's will and to guide them back to faith.

✴ Does the Torah help to differentiate between good deeds and bad deeds?

   a) **Yes**

   b) No

In Genesis 15, Abraham's faith is accounted for righteousness, and so we can say that every deed that is done without faith is sin. For example, when Joseph's brothers sinned against him by selling him to slavery in Egypt, they did this out of lack of faith. This is also true for the Hebrews who lived in Egypt and who did not believe in Moses.

God gave the people of Israel the Torah *after* the Exodus from Egypt (the first redemption), meaning the Holy One did not give the people of Israel the Torah in order for them to be redeemed. It is important that we understand the meaning of the order of events and what they represent. It can be said, that by keeping the commandments of the Torah it is impossible to be saved, and Shaul explained this by saying: **"Therefore, from works of the Law not will be justified any human flesh before Him"** (Romans 3:20). God redeemed the children of Israel from slavery in Egypt through the blood of the lamb, the Passover sacrifice. Only after the children of Israel were redeemed, God gave them the Torah. There is meaning to the fact that the giving of the Torah happened exactly fifty days after the exodus from Egypt, since the number fifty is connected to the idea of liberty: "And you shall consecrate the fiftieth year, and proclaim liberty throughout the land to all its inhabitants" (Leviticus 25:10). We must understand that freedom isn't given to us that we be free to do according to our own will, but to be able to *choose* to serve God and do His will, which the Torah teaches us to do.

✴ In order for the people of Israel to be able to be an assembly of righteous people, God gave them:

   a) Manna in the desert

   b) Torah

   c) Victory over Egypt

   d) **No correct answer**

Only whoever was redeemed by the Passover sacrifice, can walk in God's ways, that is, to leave Egypt. It is important to understand what is written in the Torah about the exodus from Egypt and the giving of the Torah, since these things were intended to indicate the future, true Redemption to come through the **Messiah our Righteousness**, Yeshua from Nazareth. In the New Covenant, Shaul emphasized the fact that the Torah has two purposes: first, to bring to our conscience the sin in our lives, as written: **For through Torah comes knowledge of sin"** (Romans 3:20), or in other words, the Torah reveals to those who read it the need for Redemption. The second goal is to show people the lifestyle that they are called to live. There is much similarity between these two goals, because when someone studies what God expects from people, he understands the need for forgiving of sins—redemption.

✱ Today there is no place for the Torah among those who have received the Gospel.

    a) True

    b) False

Even though the Torah can show a person his sins, only a believer in Messiah Yeshua can apply the righteousness of the Torah to his life. Why? Before someone is saved through faith in the Gospel, by means of the work of Yeshua, he is enslaved to sin and unable to be free from this spiritual bondage by his own strength. As we have seen earlier, the history of the people of Israel symbolizes the spiritual status of every person. Accordingly, the Israelites, while they were still slaves to Pharaoh, were unable to leave Egypt without God's help. On the other hand, after someone has received the message of the Gospel in faith, a spiritual change takes place with physical and spiritual consequences. Shaul taught about this change:

> **So that, if anyone is in Messiah, (he is) a new creation. The old has passed away; behold, having become new all things. (2 Corinthians 5:17)**

In other words, any believer in Yeshua is a new person. In fact, in another place in the New Covenant, Shaul the Apostle even used the expression "the old man" in order to describe the person who is saved. It is important to understand that there are two main consequences of the salvation experience:

a) Receiving the privilege to enter the Kingdom of God.

b) The potential to live according to God's will.

Regarding the latter, Shaul commanded the believers:

> **You are to put off, the former manner of life, the old man, which is being corrupted according to the deceitful desires, and to be renewed in the spirit of your minds, and to put on the new man, in the likeness of God, having been created in true righteousness and holiness. (Ephesians 4:22–24)**

These verses can be understood in great detail about God's plan for each person. We must remember that these words, which Shaul taught, are intended for believers alone! Only believers have the Holy Spirit among them, Who gives them the necessary supernatural power in order to apply what is said above to their lives. In the end of the passage quoted above it is written: **"The new man, in the likeness of God, having been created in true righteousness and holiness."** The purpose of this verse is to teach the reader that only through faith in Yeshua can God's will for the creation of man be manifested. It isn't by chance that Shaul used the Torah's language, as appears in Genesis, when he said: **"In the likeness of God"** (see Genesis 1:26). Later in the same verse are the words: **"In true righteousness and holiness,"** according to which whoever received forgiveness of sins, through faith in Messiah Yeshua, and became a new and spiritual person, receives also a new and an additional meaning to the Torah. Why? (**"For we know that the Torah is spiritual, but I am of the flesh, sold under sin"**). This means that until one is saved and becomes a spiritual man, he cannot completely take on the Torah as a way of life, just understand through it that he sins and needs salvation.

✸ The Torah has two goals: One is for people who have yet to believe in Yeshua, the other is for people who have already received Him as their personal Redeemer.

   a) **True**

   b) False

Shaul dealt with this issue in his epistle to the Romans:

> There is no therefore now condemnation for those who are in Messiah Yeshua. Not according to flesh they walk, according to the Spirit. For the law of the Spirit of life in Messiah Yeshua has set you free from the law of sin and of the death. For powerless is the Torah in that it was weak through the flesh. God, of Himself, sent His Son in the likeness of sinful flesh and for sin, He condemned sin in the flesh. In order that the righteousness of the Torah should be fulfilled in us, the ones not according to flesh walk, but according to the Spirit. For the ones according to flesh, the things of the flesh they think. But those ones according to Spirit, the things of the Spirit. For the mind of the flesh (is) death; but, the mind of the Spirit (is) life and peace. Hence, the mind of the flesh is enmity towards God, to the Law of God it is not subject, for it cannot be. And those being in the flesh, to please God, they are not able. (Romans 8:1–8)

From these verses, we can see that Shaul attests to the fact that those who received the gospel will not be found guilty in the eyes of God. The expression "not under the law of the Torah" expresses this idea differently. A question arises: What is the reason that people who received the Gospel won't be judged? In order to answer this question we must remember that the Torah's punishment is death. In Romans 6:8 it is written: **"But if we have died with Messiah, we believe that also we will live with Him."** Part of receiving Yeshua as our Messiah and Redeemer means that we receive the sacrifice that He made for us for once and for all. Similar to a person whose sins were forgiven by sacrificing in the Temple, so does a believer in Yeshua believe that He paid the price with His death.

In the previous chapter we quoted a passage from Jeremiah 31, where the Prophet describes the new covenant to be made with Israel and all of the nations:

> **Behold the days are coming, declares the LORD, and I will cut with the house of Israel and with the house of Judah a New Covenant. Not as the covenant which I cut with their fathers in the day I took them by the hand to bring them out from the land of Egypt, which they broke My covenant, and I was a husband to them, declares the LORD. For this is the covenant which I will cut with the house of Israel after those days, declares the LORD I place My Torah in their midst and upon their heart I wrote it and I will be to them God and they shall be to Me for a people. A man will not teach anymore his friend nor a man his brother saying, 'Know the LORD', for all of them shall know Me, from the least of them unto the greatest of them, declares the LORD because I will forgive their iniquity and their sins I will remember no more. (Jeremiah 31:31-34)**

As believers of Messiah Yeshua, we must understand that part of receiving Yeshua's forgiveness in our lives means that today His Torah is written on our hearts. In addition, God gave us the Holy Spirit Who gives us the ability to live by the spirit and not by the flesh—to listen to God's will and not to the evil inclination. It is written: **"For the law of the Spirit of life in Messiah Yeshua has set you free from the law of sin and of the death"** (Romans 8:2). We must pay attention to the expression "the Law (Torah) of the Spirit of life"—by living life by the guidance of the Holy Spirit, believers can obey God's Word and not live or behave like sinners. Shaul used in this verse two concepts: "the Torah of the Spirit of life" and "the Torah of sin and death," which represent the only two ways available to us. As we have learned, since the sin of the Tree of Knowledge, all of humanity is born to the Torah of sin and death. Only through faith in Messiah Yeshua can we live by the Torah of the Spirit of life.

It is important to clarify that despite the fact that the word "Torah" appears several times in the verse that we have quoted, it does **not** have to do with the Torah of Moses, but about a way of life. However, in the next verse the word "Torah" does mean the Torah of Moses: **"For powerless is the Torah in that it was weak through the flesh. God, of Himself, sent His Son in the likeness of sinful flesh and for sin, He condemned sin in the flesh"** (Romans 8:3).

According to Shaul, the Torah of Moses does not have the power to change the condition of humanity. Shaul is explaining to us that as a result of being sinful people, the power of the Torah is weakened by the flesh, but not because of a fault in the Torah itself. When one believes in Messiah Yeshua and receives the Holy Spirit, he is made into a vessel through which the Torah's justice is truly revealed, as written in the next verse in Romans: **"In order that the righteousness of the Torah should be fulfilled in us, the ones not according to flesh walk, but according to the Spirit"** (Romans 8:4).

From this verse we learn that the Holy Spirit will guide the believer according to the Torah's righteousness. Before someone comes to faith in Yeshua, all his thoughts are only by the flesh, and he cannot submit to God's will, as written: **"Hence, the mind of the flesh is enmity towards God, to the Law of God it is not subject, for it cannot be."** (Romans 8:7). Submitting to God means to refuse any instruction that is not based in God's teaching. On the other hand, when someone is saved, his thoughts change by the Holy Spirit, Who guides him to want to live in accordance with the righteousness of the Torah. So how should we, followers of Yeshua, live today according to Torah?

Since the destruction of the Second Temple until today, there is a change in the state of Torah. It is important to note that without the Temple it is impossible to keep the Torah. This fact isn't accidental, but points at the plan and will of God, as written in Hosea's prophecy:

> **For many days the Children of Israel will dwell without king and without prince, and without sacrifice, and without pillar, and without ephod or without Teraphim. Afterwards, the children of Israel shall return and seek the LORD their God, and David their king, and they will fear to the LORD and His goodness in the Last Days. (Hosea 3:4–5)**

The commentators agree that Hosea prophesied about the period of time that started from the destruction of the Second Temple and until the Last Days. From this prophecy we learn that throughout this period, the Torah has a different purpose. Without the Temple, more than 250 out of 613 commandments cannot be kept. It is important that the reader understand that the Torah is considered as one unit. In order to stress this point, the sages ruled that if a Torah scroll has even one mistake, the entire scroll is invalid. Ya'akov (James) the Apostle also taught this principle:

> **For whoever the whole Torah will keep, but fails in one (mitzvah/ commandment) has become of all guilty. (James 2:10)**

✦ Does someone have better odds of entering God's Kingdom if he kept all of the Torah but failed in one, as opposed to someone else who sinned very much?

  a) Yes

  b) No

Now we can understand the verse: **"And because in Torah, no one is justified (is made to be righteous) before God, (it is) evident; 'Because the righteous by faith will live'"** (Galatians 3:11). When a person tries to find justification by the Torah, by only keeping the commandments, in the end he will be found guilty. In the New Covenant there is an expression that appears about ten times, translated as "under the Law (Torah)" (ὑπὸ νόμον). Most people understand that the expression means someone subject to the authority of Torah, while Shaul used this expression slightly differently. The meaning, according to Shaul, is that everyone who is under or subject to the authority of Torah (for justification), has one fate—death—eternal separation from God. As we have already learned, this price has been paid by Yeshua's death for everyone who believes in His death and resurrection.

If we died for the Torah, are we dismissed from living according to it? Before we study how one can live by the righteousness of the Torah and apply it to his life, we must try to to understand how the rabbis see the time period we live in today (from the destruction of the Second Temple until today) versus how the New Covenant sees the same period. According to the sages, **rabbinic commandments** (not Biblical commandments) are required today until the building of the Third Temple. Although biblical commandments are studied today, without a Temple they cannot be kept. However, as Yeshua's *talmidim* we walk by the light of the Word of the living God and not by the wisdom of man (rabbinic commandments).

Yeshua taught this:

> The Law and the Prophets (were) until John; from then, the King-
> dom of God is preached, and everyone into it forces. (Luke 16:16)

We must be careful not to understand this verse wrong. The correct interpretation is that Yochanan the Immerser declared the main purpose of the Scriptures—unity with God through redemption, which is part of the Messiah's first purpose. Additionally, Yochanan called that it is time to answer this Good News. The end of the verse says: **"And everyone into it forces (God's Kingdom)."** From here we learn that the main principle of the Hebrew Scriptures is entering the Kingdom of God, and that the Torah and Prophets declare in a unanimous voice how important this matter is, so that every worthy person who discovers this enters the Kingdom.

Shaul gave us an additional verse made to clear this matter up: **"For Messiah is the end of the Torah"** (Romans 10:4). Unfortunately, many believers and theologians choose to interpret this verse wrong, saying that faith in Yeshua brings an end to the Torah. It is important to know that in the original language, the word translated as "end" (*telos*) means in this context, "goal" or "purpose." In English we can actually keep the translation the same, as the word "end" also has this meaning, as in the expression "the means to an end." One could say in fact that the Torah is the means of arriving at the end—faith in the Messiah. In other words, the Holy One gave us the Torah that we be aware our sins and search for redemption through the Righteous Messiah. If the correct interpretation of the above verse was the *end of the Torah*, and everything that it infers, there would be a contradiction with Shaul's previous words: **"In order that the righteousness of the Torah should be fulfilled in us, the ones not according to flesh walk, but according to the Spirit,"** from which we see the deep connection between the Holy Spirit and the Torah of God.

The next verse is very important since it is meant to help us understand the meaning of the Torah regarding believers today and our new status:

> But now we have been released from the Torah, having died to
> that which we were bound , in order that we serve in the newness
> of the Spirit and not in the oldness of the letter. (Romans 7:6)

The first thing that appears here is **"now we have been released from the Torah."** It is a mistake to think that the sentence means that there is no more meaning to the Torah. We must pay attention to the fact that he then says: "having died." Why does Shaul write this in this context? In order to teach the reader that believers are released from the *punishment* of the Torah—spiritual death. How are we freed from death? Because we died with the Messiah. It is a mistake to interpret this verse as if believers are freed from the truth found in the Torah. The expression "having died" refers to Yeshua's death on the cross and we, His disciples, died together with Him.

In the second half of the verse we can arrive at the right understanding, if as Yeshua's students we remember that we have the responsibility to seek and study the Word of God and its meaning according to the truth within it. It is regrettable to know that there are translations which by reading, we may reach different conclusions than the original intention of Scripture. For example, the translation "released from the Torah" causes many to arrive at the conclusion that the Torah does not have any place in the life of a believer. In order to clear up this point we shall first interpret this verse:

> But now (after believing in Yeshua as the Messiah) we are released from the Torah (from the punishment of the Torah, that is the judgment and eternal damnation), having died (with Yeshua) to that which bound us (the power of sin in the evil inclination), so that we serve in the new way of the Spirit (by the direction and strength of the Holy Spirit in our lives we can serve God and obey His will), and not simply paying attention the old way of the written law (according to the flesh).

✱ According to Yeshua, as long as I have not murdered someone I have kept the commandment, "You shall not murder," even if I have hate in my heart toward that person (see Matthew 5:21–22).

   a) True

   b) False

Summary

In the beginning of the chapter we set before us the challenge of trying to understand the Torah's role in the context of salvation. We learned that the Torah is not a tool that can grant salvation, but is meant to show the reader the need for salvation. We have seen that many things can be learned from the Torah: discerning between good and evil—God's will (good) as opposed to the will of the flesh (evil), and in addition, that the Torah is spiritual and beneficial for students of Messiah Yeshua.

Accordingly, how must we, as Yeshua's disciples, apply the Torah in our lives?

   a) Every believer must study **all** the Holy Scriptures from Genesis to Revelation.

   b) The believer needs to pray to God asking to show him, through the Holy Spirit, how he must apply His word to his life.

CHAPTER 7

1) Is there a connection between Abraham's covenant and the Torah of Moses?

   a) Yes

   b) No

2) Abraham's covenant was meant for _____.

   a) Jews

   b) Gentiles

   d) Both Jews and Gentiles

   e) None of the above

3) According to the Apostle Shaul, which of the following can be found in the foundation of Abraham's covenant?

   a) Observation of commandments

   b) Sacrifices

   c) Good deeds

   d) The Messiah

4) Despite the fact that many people think that by observing commandments one can be saved, the truth is that the Torah was given to those who:

   a) Believe

   b) Were already saved

   c) A + B

   d) Were considered Jews

5) Only those who were redeemed through the Passover sacrifice were able to:

   a) Leave Egypt

   b) Be part of God's people

   c) A + B

   d) None of the above

6) One of the Torah's roles is to reveal sins to:

    a) The public

    b) Our conscience

    c) Judges, in order to punish us

    d) None of the above

7) Anyone who believes in Yeshua as Messiah becomes:

    a) A priest

    b) A new man

    c) Someone who has left the people of Israel

    d) A small god

8) What are the two main results of faith in Messiah Yeshua?: 1) The merit to enter the Kingdom of Heaven, 2) The ability to obey God's will, 3) To be rich and without worries in this world.

    a) 1 + 2

    b) 1 + 3

    c) 2 + 3

9) Only by _____ can a person manifest God's will for humanity.

    a) Observing the commandments

    b) The Torah of Moses

    c) Good deeds

    d) Faith in Yeshua

10) The Torah is spiritual and therefore only believers in Yeshua have the ability to fully live by it.

    a) True

    b) False

11) What is the meaning of the expression: "not under the Torah"?

    a) There is no more meaning for the Torah

    b) Believers are not judged by the Torah

    c) A + B

    d) None of the above

12) When Yeshua died on the tree, all believers spiritually died together with Him. Afterwards, there is no more _____ on judgment day for us.

    a) Hope

    b) Punishment

    c) Prayer

    d) None of the above

13) Since the Torah is spiritual, it has the authority to bring change to:

    a) Humanity

    b) The people of Israel

    c) Believers

    d) All of the above

14) The Torah leads the believer in one direction and the Holy Spirit leads the believer:

    a) In a different direction

    b) In a better direction

    c) In the same direction

    d) B + C

15) Is the Torah still in force today?

    a) Yes

    b) No

16) Faith in Messiah releases the believer from the Torah. What is the meaning of this expression?

    a) From the punishment of Torah

    b) From anything that has to do with the Torah

    c) A + B

    d) None of the above

17) The goal of the Torah is:

    a) Observing mitzvot

    b) Doing good deeds

    c) Recognizing God's grace, the Messiah, and entering the Kingdom of Heaven.

    d) A + B

1) Yes

2) C

3) D

4) C

5) C

6) B

7) B

8) A

9) D

10) True

11) B

12) D

13) C

14) C

15) No

16) A

17) C

FESTIVALS OF ISRAEL

Festivals of Israel occupy an important place in Scripture. The festivals were given to us in order to remember God—His greatness, strength, loyalty, and grace. Usually, each festival has to do with a specific event that occurred in the past that God has commanded us to remember. Even though the holidays remind us of the events of the past, they have a message for the future as well. Shaul wrote regarding the Jewish holidays:

> Therefore let no one judge on you in of food or in drink, or in regard to a festival or a new moon or a Sabbath. Which are a shadow of the things to come, but the body belongs of the Messiah. (Colossians 2:16–17)

Why did Shaul open with the words: "Therefore let no one judge you ..."? In order to teach the reader that God didn't give His people the festivals (or the laws of kashrut) in order to use them as tools for judgment. The festivals, like all 613 commandments, were given in order to help us walk with God.

The goal of this chapter is to explain the main principles of each festival. In Leviticus chapter 23 we find a list of all of the biblical festivals. Though most festivals happen once a year, the first festival mentioned is a weekly festival—the Sabbath.

✱ The festivals of Israel were meant to remind us **only** of an event that happens in the past:

a) True

b) False

> And the LORD spoke to Moses saying, "Speak to the Children of Israel and you shall say to them, 'The appointed times of the LORD, which you shall proclaim them Holy Convocations, these

are My appointed times. Six days you are to do work and on the seventh day a Sabbath of rest, a holy convocation, all work you shall not do, it is a Shabbat to the LORD in all your dwelling places.'" (Leviticus 23:1–3)

God calls the festivals "the appointed times of the LORD". The word translated as appointed times here is מועד/*mo'ed* in the original Hebrew. מועד is based on the root word יעד, "objective/designation," from which we can infer that God has a purpose for each appointed time. From what follows we learn in general the purpose of each festival: "that you shall proclaim as holy convocations." The festivals are related to holiness, and God's goal is to bring holiness through these festivals to those who observe them. It is important to point out that the appointed feasts are called "holy convocations" since people are called to come together to celebrate. In Hebrew מקראי קודש, *miqraei qodhesh* comes from the root קרא, "to call." The word מועד/ *mo'ed* (appointed time) is also related to עדות/*edut*, "testimony." Accordingly, any person who faithfully keeps the festival bears witness to others on the festival and its meaning.

---------------------------------- **Shabbat** ----------------------------------

God created the universe in six days, and on the seventh day He ceased from all of His work. According to Leviticus 23, God commands us to cease work on the seventh day, since the seventh day of the week has special meaning, which God determined. There are those who think that the idea behind the mitzva of Shabbat is a day of rest, which isn't necessarily related to the seventh day, but could happen any day of the week. Yet, in Genesis 2:3 we read clearly: **"So God blessed the seventh day and made it holy, because on it God rested from all His work that He created to do."** From this verse we learn that God sanctified, designated, and set apart the seventh day from the rest of the days. Additionally, God gave the seventh day another meaning by sanctifying it.

As we have seen, the Holy One created the universe in six days, creating man on the sixth day. Why did God choose to cease from all of His work after creating Man? Because the creation of the universe testifies for God's great love for man. His love is so great that He chose to cease from all of His work to be with humanity and for them to be with Him.

There are many people who chose Sunday as a special day. This is a personal choice that any person can make, but it is important to understand that Sunday, or any other day, cannot replace the appointed time that God designated as the Sabbath day—or in other words, Saturdays. Is it possible that due to Yeshua's resurrection on Sunday that God changed His mind and now Shabbat moved from Saturday to Sunday? Did the fact that the first disciples gathered together on Sunday for various reasons, like studies, connection and worshiping God, cause a change in the purpose of Shabbat? The first *talmidim* never called Sunday Shabbat. In 1 Corinthians 16:1–2 we read:

> And concerning the collection for the saints: as I directed the churches of Galatia, so you also are to do. On the first day of every week, each of you by himself is to put something aside and store it up, as he may prosper, so that there will not when I come be collections.

Shaul's intention in these verses is to teach that the collecting of money should be done on the first day of the week. In that time period people received their salaries every day. Shaul teaches here that we must give back to God from the first fruits, the first paycheck, and not what we have leftover at the end of the week. Accordingly, this has nothing to do with Shabbat, and by Sunday being the first day of the week, it makes it even more clear that the preceding day is the true Shabbat.

Is Shabbat the only day of the week intended for worship of God? No! Every new day is a worthy day to serve and worship the LORD. For example, in Daniel 6:11, Daniel prayed three times every day. What makes Shabbat special and different from the other days of the week is that God forbade any work on this day. We chose not to explain in this book what exactly work (מלאכה/*melachah*) is, but we want to emphasize that Shabbat is the seventh day, Saturday, and that God gave this day to His people that they not busy themselves with material and worldly worries, but rather turn to Him and focus on Him and His word, as written:

> If you turn back from Shabbat your foot (from) doing your desires on My holy day, and you call the Sabbath a delight to sanctify the honorable LORD, and honor Him from doing your way and from finding your desire and speaking (your) word, then you will delight yourself in the LORD and I will cause you to ride upon the high places of the earth and I will feed you the inheritance of Jacob your father, for the mouth of the LORD has spoken. (Isaiah 58:13–14)

We can see the Sabbath as a day that God intended and for His people to disconnect from this world, and enjoy closeness with Him and renew their faith in Him. Over the course of the week we are easily distracted and we often lose the real meaning of our lives, due to thoughts and worries that come from our commitments in this world, which cause us to forget our commitment to God. We can see the Sabbath as a gift that we have received from God, a day in which we are free from the worries of the world and can focus on God and His Word. As a result of the renewal of the mind and spirit over the course of Shabbat we are better prepared for the new week.

✷ The main goal of the Sabbath commandments is to rest one day of the week.

True/**False**

THE SPRING FESTIVALS

Passover and the Festival of Matzot

The Scriptures teach us that Passover is connected to redemption. It is important to understand that "Passover" refers to a specific date, the 14th day of Nisan, when the Passover sacrifice was sacrificed:

> These are the appointed times of the LORD, holy proclamations which you shall proclaim them in their appointed times. In the first month, on the fourteenth day of the month, at twilight, is the LORD's Passover. (Leviticus 23:4–5)

✷ Is there a connection between blood and redemption? **Yes**

Throughout the Holy Scriptures we see a direct connection between blood and redemption. In the story of the exodus from Egypt it is important to understand the meaning of the blood of the Passover sacrifice:

> And it shall be that the blood is to you for a sign upon the houses which you there and I will see the blood and I will pass over you and there will not be a plague of destruction when I strike the land of Egypt. (Exodus 12:13)

Only by merit of the blood of the Passover lamb, God's judgment didn't come upon those who kept the Passover in Egypt. In the New Testament we find a parallel: Shaul revealed to us that "Messiah, our Passover lamb, has been sacrificed" (1 Corinthians 5:7). Meaning that in the same way that the Israelites left from bondage in Egypt to experience liberty, by merit of the lamb's blood that was a sign upon their houses, so too, those who have faith in Yeshua the Messiah (the Lamb of God) go free (redemption) from slavery (sin) through the forgiveness of sins, by which we are now free to serve God instead of sin. This is the power of redemption. We can now understand that the story of the Exodus from Egypt points to the future. The Passover is actually a preparation for the Festival of Matzot as written:

> And on the fifteenth day of this month is the Feast of Unleavened Bread to the LORD; seven days you shall eat unleavened bread. On the first day, a holy will be for you; all ordinary work you shall not do. You will offer a fire offering to the LORD for seven days. On the seventh day is a holy convocation, all ordinary work, you shall not do. (Leviticus 23:6-8)

On the Feast of Unleavened Bread there are several important hints that point out the need for redemption. For example, the main thing we learn about the matza is that there is no leaven in it. According to the tradition of the Jewish people and what is written in the New Covenant, there is a direct correlation between leaven and sin. In this context Shaul wrote:

> Not good your boasting. Do you not know that a little leaven, the whole lump leavens? Therefore clean out the old leaven that you may be a new lump, as you are unleavened. For also our Passover Lamb, on behalf of us, has been sacrificed—Messiah. So that we keep the festival, not with the old leaven, the leaven of malice and evil, but with the unleavened bread of sincerity and truth. (1 Corinthians 5:6-8)

If so, what is the connection between the Passover and the Festival of Matzot? The Passover sacrifice is deliverance which brings us to redemption, while the Festival of Matzot teaches us what we must do after we have been saved—to truly repent and turn from a life of sin. In other words, the Festival of Unleavened Bread reveals to the believer the call to walk in God's ways and not to continue to serve the evil intention.

✦ Is there a correlation between the Passover, the Festival of Unleavened Bread, and the worship of God? **Yes**/No

Afterward Moses and Aaron came and they said to Pharaoh, "Thus said the LORD, the God of Israel, 'Send forth My people, that they may hold a feast to Me in the desert" (Exodus 5:1).

From this verse we see that the Holy One took the Israelites out of Egypt for a defined purpose: that the Israelites remember, serve, and thank God in the desert for their redemption.

✱ According to the Torah, does "the Passover" refer to all seven days of the festival? Yes/**No**

During the Festival of Matzot, a very important time period starts, which is called the counting of the Omer. This period always starts on the Sunday after the Sabbath of the week of the Festival of Unleavened Bread.

> **And the LORD spoke to Moses saying, "Speak to the Children of Israel and say to them, 'When you come into the land which I am giving to you, you shall harvest the harvest and you shall bring the first omer of your harvest to the priest and he shall wave the omer before the LORD for your will, from the day after the Sabbath the priest shall wave it.'" (Leviticus 23:9–11)**

It is important to note that the first day of this period does not have a set day. The reason is that the first day of the count must be on a Sunday. This day is called "firstfruits." Shaul connected this day to Yeshua's resurrection:

> **But now, Messiah has been raised from the dead, the firstfruits of those who have fallen asleep. For because through a man (came) death, also through a man, the resurrection of the dead. For as in Adam all die, so also in Messiah will all be made alive. But each in his own order: Messiah the firstfruits, then those of Messiah at His coming. (1 Corinthians 15:20–23)**

It is not by chance that Shaul used the word "firstfruits" in connection with the Resurrection. The commandment for the first day of the Omer, which means sheaf, is as written: "You shall bring the sheaf of the firstfruits of your harvest to the priest." After the priest/*kohen* receives the "sheaf of the firstfruits of your harvest," it says "He shall wave the sheaf before the LORD for your will. " The meaning of this commandment is that a person chooses the best part (firstfruits) and brings it to the *kohen*, out of hope that the rest of his harvest will be as good as the firstfruits. The *kohen*'s service is to wave the firstfruits and the intention of this action is declaration of victory. This is the meaning of "for your will", that is, the Holy One will accept our desire for victory over sin and we will experience resurrection power and be like Messiah at His coming . What is this victory? Yeshua arose from the dead on this day in order to reveal to us that He triumphed over sin (death) for the believers, and in the future we will also be like Him, completely freed from sin.

✦ What is the Sunday after the Sabbath during the Festival of Unleavened Bread?

    a) A holy convocation

    b) Firstfruits

    c) The day we start the counting of the 'Omer

    d) B + C

The Festival of Shavu'ot (Pentecost)

According to the commandment of the Counting of the Omer, one must count both seven weeks and fifty days:

> **And you shall count for yourselves from the day after the Sabbath, from the day you brought the omer for waving there shall be seven full weeks; until the day after the seventh Sabbath, you shall count fifty days and you shall offer a new grain offering to the LORD. (Leviticus 23:15–16)**

There are those who say that this counting attests for expectation toward something. According to the tradition, at the end of this period, God gave the people of Israel the Ten Commandments, which is the base for the entire Torah. Just as the Passover isn't connected only to the past, but also prophesies the future, so too, is Shavuot (i.e., Pentecost).

> **And in the fulfilling (the count for) the day of Pentecost, they were all together in same place. And came suddenly out of heaven a sound like a rushing wind, violent; and it filled all the house where they were sitting. And appeared to them divided tongues as fire and He sat on each one of them. And they were all filled with the Holy Spirit and began to speak in other tongues just as the Spirit gave them utterance. (Acts 2:1–4)**

It can be said that the period of the latter days started from that Shavuot when the Holy Spirit alighted upon those who believed in Messiah Yeshua. We must understand that the idea "אחרית הימים," the end of days, or more accurately, the latter days, refers to two different periods: The first period started on that festival of Shavuot and will end in the Second Coming of the Messiah. This will be when the Messiah returns to this world to establish the Kingdom of God. The second period refers to the common usage of this concept, the three and a half last years before the Messiah's return to this world (Daniel spoke about the last week [שבועים instead of שבועות, this is a hint that he is referring to years and not days] and these seven years are split into two equal parts). How can it be that the same term refers to two different periods? It is interesting to see that Shim'on Keifa (Peter) spoke about the end of days on Shavuot, when the Holy Spirit alighted upon the believers:

> But Peter, standing with the eleven, lifted up his voice and spoke for to them: Men of Judea and the ones dwelling in Jerusalem, to all, let this be known to you, and give heed to my words. For not as you have received, these people are not drunk, for it is only the third hour of the day. But this is what was said through the prophet Joel:
>
> "And it will be in the last days, God says, that I will pour out from My Spirit upon all flesh, and your sons and your daughters will prophesy, and your young men will see visions, and your old men will dream dreams; and even on my male servants and female servants in those days I will pour out from my Spirit, and they will prophesy.
>
> "And I will give wonders in the heavens above and signs on the earth below, blood, and fire, and vapor of smoke; the Sun will turned to darkness and the moon into blood, before comes the Day of the Lord, the great and magnificent day.
>
> "And it will be that all who calls upon the Name of the Lord will be saved." (Acts 2:14–20)

Shim'on Keifa knew that these words from Yoel's prophecy originally refer to the last three-and-a-half years prior to the Kingdom (see Daniel chapter 9). Why then, did Keifa use this quote regarding the festival of Shavuot? Since he wanted to teach those who heard him that the time has come to prepare the Kingdom of God. At the same time, it is important to point out that only a small part of this prophecy was manifested in Keifa's days.

The Prophet Isaiah also spoke about the gift of the Holy Spirit:

> "And will come to Zion a Redeemer, who turns away transgression in Jacob," declares the LORD. "And as for Me, this is My covenant with them," said the LORD: "My Spirit Who is upon you, and My words which I have put in your mouth, will not depart out of your mouth, or out of the mouth of your offspring, or out of the mouth of your children's offspring," said the LORD, "from now and forevermore." (Isaiah 59:20–21)

These two prophets prophesied on the gift of the Holy Spirit in the end of days. Why then, did Shim'on Keifa speak about them almost two thousand years ago? For it is clear to all that the last three-and-a-half years were not in Keifa's days. The answer is in order to teach that the Holy Spirit was given also to those who recognized the Messiah and received Him when He came to the world the first time. The Holy Spirit is given to believers in Yeshua so that through His help and direction we may be prepared for the Kingdom and His return to Zion.

The giving of the Holy Spirit is also called the "guarantee of the Spirit":

> Who is the guarantee of our inheritance, for the redemption of the obtaining possession, to the praise of His glory. (Ephesians 1:14)

> The One also having sealed us and has given us the guarantee of His Spirit in our hearts. (2 Corinthians 1:22)

The expression "guarantee of the Spirit" shows an additional role of the Holy Spirit, that has to do with the promise of our final redemption.

✴ The believers received the Holy Spirit as a _____ regarding the promise of the future to come.

   a) Hope

   b) **Guarantee**

   c) Encouragement

   d) Message

In Acts, we read about countless miracles and wonders that were done by the Apostles through the Holy Spirit as proof that Yeshua is the promised Messiah. In the

Latter Days there will once again be many miracles and wonders that God will do Himself with the goal of showing the people of Israel His greatness:

> **So that might come times of refreshing from the presence of the Lord, and that He may send the One appointed for you, Messiah Yeshua. (Acts 3:20)**

In this verse, we find the expression "times of refreshing ... from the presence of the Lord," which refers to the pouring out of the Holy Spirit at the end of this age. One must understand that since that Shavuot, when the Holy Spirit came for the first time, and until the end of days, every person who believes in Messiah Yeshua receives the Holy Spirit. If so, what is the meaning of the expression "times of refreshing may come from the presence of the Lord"? As we have learned, the receiving of the Holy Spirit the first time was related to the first coming of Yeshua. Accordingly, the "times of refreshing," the second receiving of the Holy Spirit, will be related to His second coming, as quoted above: "... **that He may send the One appointed for you, Messiah Yeshua.**" During this time there will be a great repentance among the people of Israel who will recognize and accept Yeshua as their Messiah and many Gentiles.

THE AUTUMN FESTIVALS

There are different speculations on the relationship between the festivals and the Messiah. There is no doubt that the Spring Festivals are related to the first coming of the Messiah, and therefore many are of the opinion that the autumn festivarls are related to His second coming. This view is of course not certain, but there are hints that point to the connection between the fall festivals and the end of days.

In regard to the first Fall festival one reads,

> **And the LORD spoke to Moses, saying, "Speak to the Children of Israel, saying, In the seventh month, on the first day of the month, it will be for you a day of solemn rest, a memorial blast, a holy convocation. All ordinary work, and you shall not do, and you shall offer a fire offering to the LORD." (Leviticus 23:23–25)**

The first autumn festival is called "a memorial blast." We know this festival by the name given by the sages—Rosh HaShanah or the Hebrew New Year. The word "blast" refers to the blowing of the shofar, a ram's horn, and during the festival we read, in accordance with the tradition of the people of Israel, the story of the binding of Isaac which appears in Genesis:

> And Abraham lifted up his eyes and looked, and behold a ram, behind, caught in a thicket by his horns. And Abraham went and took the ram and offered it up as a burnt offering instead of his son. And Abraham called the name of that place, "The LORD will see"; as it is said to this day, "On the mount of the LORD it will be seen." (Genesis 22:13–14)

As is well known, God told Abraham to sacrifice his special son as a burnt offering on Mount Moriah, but the moment before Abraham sacrificed Isaac, the Angel of the LORD appeared and told him: "Do not lay your hand on the boy or do anything to him." Thanks to Abraham's faithfulness to do God's commandments, that Angel was sent to tell Abraham that God had mercy on his son's life and provided him a ram as an alternative sacrifice instead of Isaac. There is much meaning to the fact that the ram was "caught in a thicket by his horns" since shofars are made from these thorns.

The main message of these verses is that God would provide in the future an alternative sacrifice for His people, that those who receive this sacrifice will receive life. On every Day of the Blasting of Shofars, when we hear the blast of the shofar, we must remember the sacrifice that God provided people so that we receive life instead of death, through the sacrifice of Messiah Yeshua. It is important to understand that the concepts of life and death are not of the physical aspect, but of the spiritual. Accordingly, the ram symbolizes the (then) future work of the Messiah, who gave His life for the salvation of God's people.

After the Memorial of the Blowing of Shofars comes the Day of Atonement, Yom Kippur:

> And the LORD spoke to Moses, saying, "But on the tenth day of this seventh month is the Day of Atonement. A holy convocation, it will be for you, and you shall afflict yourselves and offer a fire offering to the LORD. and all work you shall not do on that very day, for it is a Day of Atonements, to make atonement for you before the LORD your God. For everyone who will not afflict [himself] on that very day shall be cut off from his people. And everyone who does any work on that very day, I will destroy that one from among his people. All work you shall not do, an eternal

> statute throughout your generations in all your dwelling places.
> It is a statute forever throughout your generations in all your
> dwelling places." (Leviticus 23:26–31)

Yom Kippur is a day intended to be sanctified (separated) for God, on which we must go over our relationship with God. The mitzva to "afflict yourselves" that was given to the people of Israel points out that in order to be able to receive atonement for our sins we must truly repent by asking for forgiveness from the LORD.

In Hebrews, it says that Yeshua is our high priest (הכהן הגדול):

> Therefore having a Great High Priest Who has passed through
> the heavens, Yeshua, the Son of God, let us hold fast confession.
> (Hebrews 4:14)

From this verse we learn that Yeshua is called the High Priest, and this fact reveals to us how great His work is and what He achieved for us—true atonement and for-giveness of sins. As believers, the Chasidim (followers) of Messiah Yeshua, though we have already received this atonement in our lives, we should not undervalue God's mercy. In order to receive Yeshua's atonement, we must prepare, and this preparation needs to include true introspection that leads us to confessing our sins and asking Messiah Yeshua to save us, to help us to truly return in repentance (לחזור בתשובה).

The next autumn festival is the Feast of Sukkot (Booths):

> And the LORD spoke to Moses saying, "Speak to the Children
> of Israel, saying, 'On the fifteenth day of this seventh month, a
> Feast of Tabernacles, seven days to the LORD. On the first day, a
> holy convocation, all ordinary work you should not do. Seven days
> you shall offer a fire offering to the LORD. On the eighth day a
> holy convocation will be for you. You shall offer a fire offering to
> the LORD. It is an assembly, all ordinary work you shall not do.'"
> (Leviticus 23:33–36)

The Feast of Sukkot is prophesied to play an important role in the Kingdom of God. The Prophet Zechariah speaks about Sukkot at the end of his prophecy:

> And it shall come about all who remain from all the nations that
> went against Jerusalem they shall go up each year to worship the

> **King, the LORD of Hosts and to celebrate the Feast of Tabernacles. (Zechariah 14:16)**

The Holy One commanded His people to sit in booths seven days in order to remember the forty years that the Israelites wandered in the desert due to lack of faith in God. On this festival we remember how God provided for all of His people's needs, despite their lack of faith and loyalty, which shows how faithful God is and the need for us to trust and have faith in Him. The people's lack of faith in God brought upon the generation in the desert, the punishment so they couldn't enter the promised land—the Land of Israel—parallel to this, God doesn't allow a person to enter His Kingdom without true faith in Messiah Yeshua.

✦ The main message of Sukkot is _____.

   a) To observe Torah

   b) To trust God

   c) To have faith in God

   d) **B + C**

The last festival in this season is Shemini Atzeret, the Eighth day of Assembly. Though we don't have much information about this holiday in the Bible, it has much meaning in Judaism. The name of this festival includes the number eight, which relates to the matter of the Kingdom (see appendix). Even though Shemini Atzeret is not part of the Feast of Sukkot, there is an obvious relationship between these festivals. According to the Ibn-Shushan dictionary, the meaning of the Hebrew word *atzeret* (עצרת) is: "An assembly of masses of a people or a multi-national gathering for the purpose of discussion or for the purpose of announcing or explaining important matters." As we have learned, in order to take part in this assembly—the Kingdom—we must believe in God and trust in Him. Now we can understand why we celebrate the Eighth day of Assembly immediately after the seven day Feast of Booths.

Chanukkah and Purim

Chanukkah (חנוכה): Many people connect the miracle of Chanukkah to the story of the oil in the Temple, but the real miracle was the military victory of the Judeans over the Greeks. The purpose of the oil miracle was to show the People of Israel God's faithfulness and that He was the cause of the great victory over the Greeks. The name of the festival, Chanukkah, means dedication, referring to the rededication of the Temple to the God of Israel, which reminds us that God is the One who gave us the victory and as a result of this, His people can worship Him in the Temple. Chanukkah is a festival in which we remember a past miracle, but it is important to see how this holiday also has to do with the future. In Haggai's prophecy we find a direct hint to Chanukkah—there is an emphasis on the date, Chanukkah eve:

> Please set your heart (pay attention) from this day and forward, from the twenty-fourth day of the ninth (month), from the day which the foundations of the sanctuary of the LORD were laid, you pay attention. (Haggai 2:18)

Why did Haggai the prophet emphasize the day that only the foundation of the Temple was laid and not the day when the Temple's construction was finished? In order to teach us that the building of the Second Temple isn't the main point about the festival of Chanukkah, since in the future Chanukkah will have a much greater meaning, and so the historical defeat over the Greeks will be small in comparison to the great victory that will be seen in the future.

> For thus said the LORD of Hosts, a little more and I am shaking the heavens and the earth and the sea and the dry land. I will shake all the nations and they shall bring the desire of all nations and I will fill this house (with) glory, said the LORD of Hosts. To Me is the silver and to Me is the gold declares the LORD of Hosts. Great will be the glory of this last Temple, more than the first, said the LORD of Hosts and in this place I will give shalom said the LORD of Hosts. (Haggai 2:6–9)

Haggai teaches us that in the future, in the latter days, God will give His people victory over all the nations. This victory will cause the nations to bring their treasures to Jerusalem, in order to fill the treasury of the Temple with silver and gold. He also says "The latter glory of this house shall be greater than the former Temple, said the LORD of hosts and in this place I will give peace, says the LORD of Hosts." It is important to pay attention to the fact it is written "this latter Temple". This verse does not point to the Second Temple that was built in the days of Haggai, but rather to the Third Temple, that will be in the future in the days when Messiah Yeshua will return.

As has been noted, the number eight is related to the Kingdom of God, accordingly there are those that wait for the Messiah to reveal Himself in one of the holidays celebrated during the eight days, either Passover + Unleavened Bread (1+7 days), Sukkot + Shemini Atzereth (7+1 days) or Chanukkah (8 days). It is interesting to note that in the New Testament there is a story about the Festival of Chanukkah:

> And it came about the dedication (the Festival of Chanukkah)
> in Jerusalem and it was winter and Yeshua was walking in the
> Temple in Solomon's Hall. Therefore, the Judeans surrounded
> Him and were saying to Him, "Until when do You lift up our souls
> (keep us in suspense)? If you You are the Messiah, say to us
> plainly." (John 10:22–24)

The Solomon's Hall was the closest place to the Sanctuary, where it was permitted for anyone who wasn't from the tribe of Levi to be. In the verses quoted above it says "Yeshua was walking in the Temple." The Greek word for walking here is περιεπάτει, *periepatei*, meaning in this usage, "walking back and forth." When Yeshua was in the hall of Solomon, the leaders surrounded Him and asked Him: "How long will you keep us in suspense? If you are the Messiah, tell us plainly." Why did they ask Yeshua this specifically during Chanukkah? As we have learned, according to our sages there are great expectations that the Messiah will reveal Himself on this festival and that's why the leaders came and asked Him about it. In the future to come, Yeshua will return and enter the Temple in order to establish His Kingdom. The obvious question is, will this event happen on Chanukkah? At the end of the book of Daniel we can find a hint:

> Blessed is the one who waits and arrives to the 1,335 days.
> (Daniel 12:12)

Earlier in the book of Daniel, we read about the last *week of years*—before God establishes His Kingdom. The Prophets divided this period into two parts: Two periods of three-and-a-half years each (למועד מועדים וחצי, two times, a time, and a half), or two periods of forty-two months or 1,260 days. In the above verse, Daniel spoke about the second half, that is after 1,260 days, but he extended the time seventy-five more days to arrive at 1,335 days. The secret here is that between Yom Kippur and Chanukkah there are exactly seventy-five days.

Purim: The Scroll of Esther relates that God is faithful to save His people from their enemies. Throughout the scroll, we see how the Holy One turned everything that the enemy planned to do against Israel, to our benefit. The climax of the story is when Esther bravely acted and said: "Then I will go to the king, though it is against the law, and when I perish, I perish." From that moment God began to change the Jews' situation. Though the Gentiles were about to destroy and kill all of the Jews, in the end:

> To the Jews there was light and gladness and joy and honor, and
> in every country and in every city and every place where the word

> of the king and his law arrived, gladness and joy for the Jews a
> banquet and a holiday and many from the peoples of the earth
> became Jews, for the fear of the Jews had fallen upon them.
> (Esther 8:16–17)

There are those who say that the situation of the people of Israel at the end of the
Scroll of Esther foreshadows the position that they will have in the Kingdom of God.

CHAPTER 8

1) The Festivals of Israel are also called:

   a) Important days

   b) Appointed times

   c) Meaningful days

   d) Days off

2) Are the Festivals of Israel also called Holy Convocations?

   a) Yes

   b) No

3) Since Yeshua was resurrected on Sunday, is the Sabbath now on Sunday?

   a) Yes

   b) No

4) On the Sabbath we have the privilege to disconnect from the worries of life, focus on God and enjoy Him.

   a) True

   b) False

5) As believers in Yeshua we declare that the Passover sacrifice is:

   a) Our prayers

   b) Good deeds

   c) The Passover Seder

   d) The Messiah

6) What does leavened bread represent?

   a) A sacrifice

   b) Pride

   c) Sin

   d) B + C

7) On the 15th of Nisan (first Biblical month) God took the Israelites out of Egypt so that they could:

   a) Do whatever they want

   b) Serve Him

   c) Establish a Jewish and democratic State

   d) Receive the Talmud

8) There is much meaning to the fact that first God saved His people from Egypt and afterward gave them the Torah.

   a) True

   b) False

9) The term "firstfruits" regards to:

   a) Resurrection

   b) Victory

   c) Harvest

   d) All of the above

10) On which day was Yeshua resurrected?

   a) We don't know

   b) The first day of the Counting of the Omer

   c) The Holiday of Shavuot

   d) It doesn't matter which day, the important thing is that He rose from the dead!

11) Which holiday is celebrated immediately after the end of the Counting of the Omer?

   a) Shavuot

   b) Beginning of the harvest

   c) 33rd of the Omer

   d) None of the above

12) According to the tradition of Israel, the giving of Torah happened on this day:

   a) Shavuot

   b) 33rd of the Omer

   c) First of Sivan

   d) First of Tishrei

13) According to the New Covenant, Yeshua first sent the Holy Spirit to the believers on the first Shavuot after He arose from the dead.

    a) True

    b) False

14) According to the Torah, the first of Tishrei is:

    a) Rosh HaShanah

    b) Yom Teru'ah (Day of the Shofar Blast)

    c) Zikaron Teru'ah (Memorial of the Shofar Blast)

    d) B + C

15) The blowing of the shofar reminds whoever hears it, what God provided for the people of Israel:

    a) A Temple

    b) A State

    c) Victory

    d) Provision

16) For how many days is the Feast of Sukkot celebrated?

    a) 3

    b) 7

    c) 8

    d) 6

17) The main miracle during Chanukkah was:

    a) The oil

    b) The victory over the Greeks

    c) The rebuilding of the Temple

    d) The building of the walls of Jerusalem in fifty-one days

ANSWERS

1) B

2) True

3) False

4) True

5) D

6) D

7) B

8) True

9) D

10) B

11) A

12) A

13) True

14) D

15) C

16) B

17) B

THE LAND OF ISRAEL—
THE BIBLICAL PROMISED LAND

The Holy One has plans to establish His Kingdom in this world, and the Land of Israel has a special role in this plan. In Genesis, God made a covenant with Abraham our Father, and in the New Covenant Shaul reveals to us that the basis of this covenant is the Messiah:

> And to Abraham were made the promises and to his Seed. It does not say, "And to seeds," as to many, but as to one, "And to your Seed," who is Messiah. (Galatians 3:16)

It is important to see that the covenant depends on an additional detail, as written:

> And the LORD said to Abram, "You go from your land and from your birthplace and from the house of your father to the land which I will show you." (Genesis 12:1)

It is clear that God commanded Abram not only to leave his land, but more importantly to arrive at "the Land that I will show you," the Land of Israel. God's call to Abram demanded faith, and we see this in chapter 15:

> And (Abram) believed the LORD, and He accounted it to him righteousness. (Genesis 15:6)

Abram's faith has many consequences. We read "and He accounted it to him righteousness," that is, Abram's faith made him righteous before the LORD; brought him into the Kingdom of God. In Judaism, the merit to enter the Kingdom of God, or the World to Come, is given through redemption (*geula,* גאולה), which means that there is a connection between faith and redemption. In the Torah, the concept of "redemption" is described while entering the Promised Land. God says to Abraham in the next verse:

> And He said to him, "I am the LORD who brought you out from Ur of the Chaldeans to give to you this land to inherit (possess) it." (Genesis 15:7)

Therefore, there is a clear connection between what is said in chapter 12 and 15. In Genesis 15:7 we see that God gives Abraham the land to possess—to him for an inheritance. Some say that the word inheritance in Hebrew, *yerusha*, ירושה, is a hint to the name of the Holy City, Jerusalem, from which the Righteous Messiah will rule in the Kingdom of God. From here we can infer that as in the past, Abraham needed to be in the Land of Israel physically, in order for God's promises to be fulfilled, so too must the Jewish people, be in the Land in order for the Kingdom of God to be established.

God repeats His plans in Chapter 17:

> I, behold My covenant with you, and you shall be a father to many nations. And your name shall no longer be called Abram, your name shall be Abraham, for a father of many nations I will appoint you. And I will make you very, very fruitful and I will appoint you that nations and kings shall go out from you. And I will establish My covenant between Me and between you and between your seed after you throughout their generations for an eternal covenant to be for you God and to your seed after you. And I will give to you and to your seed after you the land of your sojournings all the land of Canaan for an eternal possession and I will be to them God. (Genesis 17:4–8)

These verses start with a very meaningful declaration: "Behold, My covenant is with you." In Hebrew this is אני הנה בריתי איתך, and could literally be translated: "I, behold, My covenant is with you." Why does the word אני/I appear at the beginning of the sentence? It is meant to emphasize the importance of the covenant being personal between I (God) and you (Abraham). The second part of this verse says, "You shall be a father of a multitude of nations," which shows that God, through this covenant, will bring a great change in Abraham's life and not just for Abraham, but in the entire world by God acting through him. It is interesting to see that though at the time Abraham did not have even one descendant, and he was to become "a father of a multitude of nations." At the same time, for this change to happen, Abraham himself needed to change, and this is why one reads: "No longer shall your name be called Abram, but your name shall be Abraham, for I have made you the father of a multitude of nations." The fact that his name was changed, teaches the reader that Abram became a new man (Abraham). As we learned before, he believed in the LORD and He counted it to him righteousness, meaning that Abraham came into the covenant with God by faith and became a new man, a righteous man (*tzaddik*, צדיק).

The next verse says: "I will make you very, very (במאד מאד) fruitful." From this promise, we learn that the result of good and healthy relationship with God is that it allows us to bring forth much fruit (good deeds). It is interesting that the word "very" (*meod*, מאד) appears twice. The first very (מאד) refers to this world, and the second very (מאד) refers to the World to Come. This is also the meaning in verse 7 of "an everlasting covenant." The covenant between God and Abraham will eventually lead to the establishment of the Kingdom of God, which is everlasting. Then the next verse is: "And I will give to you and to your offspring after you the land of your sojournings, all the land of Canaan, for an everlasting possession, and I will be their God." The purpose of this verse is to reveal to us that the Kingdom won't come until Abraham's descendants (actually the Children of Jacob) will live in all of the Promised Land. The expression "an everlasting possession" also hints to the Kingdom of God.

✦ Even though all those who have faith in the Seed of Abraham, Messiah Yeshua, have the privilege to enter the Kingdom of God, the right to the Land of Israel belongs only to:

   a) No one has a right to the Land of Israel anymore

   b) Descendants of Jacob

   c) All believers

   d) None of the above

In the context of Abraham, the word "your seed" refers mainly to descendants of Jacob. This word has to do with God's promise to Abraham through the seed of blessing and promise—the Children of Israel. The *interpretation* of the phrase "your seed" as referring only to followers of Yeshua would contradict all of God's promises to the Israelites and the words of the Prophets regarding the People of Israel and the Land of Israel in the end of days. The Torah itself strengthens the promise as being between the People and Land of Israel. For example, in Genesis Jacob was told:

> **And he dreamed and behold a ladder was stood to the earth and its top reached the heavens and behold angels of God go up and**

> down on it. And behold the LORD stood upon it and he said, "I am
> the LORD, the God of Abraham your father and the God of Isaac,
> the land which you are lying upon it, to you I am giving it and to
> your seed, and your seed will be as the dust of the earth and you
> shall burst forth to the west and to the east and to the north
> and to the south and will be blessed in you all the families of the
> earth and in your seed. And behold I am with you and I will keep
> you in all which you go and I will bring you back to this ground
> for I will not leave you until I have done what I have spoken to
> you." (Genesis 28:12–15)

These verses are well known and there is a general agreement that the dream is a
prophecy about the Messiah's work, which is to bring on the Oneness between God
and humanity (those who are saved). Later on, Yeshua attested that He is the ladder:

> Truly, truly, I say to you, from now on you will see heaven opened,
> and the angels of God ascending and descending on the Son of
> Man. (John 1:51)

When God said to Jacob: "I am the LORD, the God of Abraham your father and the
God of Isaac." He meant to say that the covenant that He made with his forefathers
is still valid. God mentions the Land: "The land on which you lie I will give to you
and to your offspring," teaching us that one of the conditions for there to be unity
between God and man, is the fulfilling of the promise of the people of Israel living
in the Land of Israel. This complete unity ultimately refers to the Kingdom of God.
Likewise, in order for God to establish His Kingdom, the Jewish people must dwell in
the Land of Israel and "spread abroad to the west and to the east and to the north
and to the south":

> On that day the LORD cut with Abram a covenant, saying, "To
> your seed I gave this land, from the river of Egypt unto the great
> river, the river Euphrates." (Genesis 15:18)

The word "spread abroad," (*ufaratzta*, ופרצת) is important, as it is used in the same
context also in Isaiah's prophecy:

> For to the right and to the left, you will spread out, and your seed nations will possess and to desolate cities they will return. (Isaiah 54:3)

It is worth noting that in Biblical Hebrew left and right can often mean north and south, so the promise to Jacob and Isaiah's prophecy are very parallel. Isaiah's prophecy is known as an end times prophecy, the time when the Jewish people would return to the Land of Israel and to the cities and villages in which their ancestors lived. The people would also grow and possess nations from the river of Egypt to the river Euphrates.

In the end times, most of the nations will resist the State of Israel and demand that they give up parts of the inheritance that God promised them, for example the lands of Judea and Samaria. Already in our days we see how many peoples believe the lie that only if the State of Israel give up some of the Promised Land, can there be peace in our area. This approach completely contradicts the Word of God, as written: "Your offspring shall be like the dust of the earth, and you shall spread abroad to the west and to the east and to the north and to the south, and in you and your offspring shall all the families of the earth be blessed." According to Scripture, *only* when the Jewish people inherit all of the promised inheritance from God, will God bless the nations and His Kingdom be established.

The People of Israel and Exile

In Deuteronomy, Moses our teacher prophesied that the people of Israel would go into exile: "Among all the nations where the LORD your God has driven you" (Deuteronomy 30:1). The Israelites were exiled from the Promised Land because:

> And they shall go and they shall serve other gods and they shall bow down to gods which you have not known them and had no portion with them and the anger of the LORD will be in that land to bring upon it every curse written in this book and the LORD uprooted them from their land in anger and in wrath and in great indignation and He will send them to another land in this day. (Deuteronomy 29:25–27)

Throughout most of the Hebrew Scriptures the term "exile" refers to the Babylonian exile. When the people of Israel are in exile, this affects all of Israel's essence, since the Jewish identity is connected to dwelling in the Land of Israel. When the people are in exile this is a disaster in many ways, but mainly with everything related to serving God:

> How shall we sing the LORD's song upon a foreign land?
> (Psalm 137:4)

This verse isn't just an expression, but the author's true question, which requires an answer. So the psalm continues:

> If I forget you, O Jerusalem, let my right hand forget! Let my tongue stick to the my cheek, if I do not remember you, if I do not lift up Jerusalem above my highest joy! (Psalm 137:5–6)

These verses teach us that the Jewish people can never adapt themselves to a new reality in any place that is opposed to God's plan, namely, in exile. The natural place for the people of Israel is the Promised Land.

✱ We have learned that Jerusalem was always very important for Jewish individuals who have faith in God. Likewise, believers in Yeshua need to understand and accept the importance of Jerusalem, so that they can benefit from the connection between Jerusalem and:

a) Heaven

b) The Kingdom of God that is to come

c) The Assembly of Elders in Babylon

d) The UN

At the heart of the *Amidah* prayer, there are several phrases regarding the final redemption:

> Cause us to return, our Father, to Your Torah; draw us near, our King, to Your service; and bring us back to You in whole-hearted repentance. Blessed are You LORD, who desires penitence.
>
> Pardon us, our Father, for we have sinned; forgive us, our King, for we have transgressed; for You are a good and forgiving God. Blessed are You LORD, gracious One who pardons abundantly.

> O behold our affliction and wage our battle; redeem us speedily for the sake of Your Name, for You God are the mighty redeemer. Blessed are You LORD, Redeemer of Israel.
>
> Sound the great shofar for our freedom; raise a banner to gather our exiles, and bring us together from the four corners of the earth into our land. Blessed are You LORD, who gathers the dispersed of His people Israel.

These prayers were written by our sages, but we can clearly see that they are based on the Holy Scripture and we can find in them the foundation of redemption. We read: "Cause us to return, our Father, to Your Torah." This request means that the Children of Israel must return to God's Word and revelation. Until the people of Israel understand that the only way to the true life of faith is in the Holy Scriptures, they won't spiritually change. God's people will continue to live in exile both physically and spiritually and suffer from being distant from God. It is not by chance that we read immediately in the next sentence, "draw us near, our King, to Your service." Only through God's Word can we be faithful to God's will and serve Him properly. Only after one understands these things can he repent, which is the end of the first request: "and bring us back to You in whole-hearted repentance." No one can bring himself to a state of true repentance without God's help, since part of full repentance is truly submitting oneself to the authority of Scripture.

Only a true repentance, together with the will to serve God, can lead to asking Him for forgiveness: "Pardon us, our Father, for we have sinned; forgive us, our King, for we have transgressed." The intention to leave evil is a big part of repentance.

Once we have repented, according to God's will, we can see God's hand working in every aspect of our lives, including everything related to protection from our enemies. And thus the prayer continues: "Behold our affliction and wage our battle." Parallel to the Israelites' situation in Egypt, the people of Israel cannot leave exile without God's help. The prayer continues: "Redeem us speedily for the sake of Your Name." Redemption never came to the people of Israel as something they earned. Throughout the history of God's relationship with the people of Israel we see that the redemption of His people is always a result of God's mercy, faithfulness, and for the sake of His name. The expression "for the sake of Your Name" is very meaningful and shows us how God turns toward His people in mercy and forgiveness in order to return Israel to His will.

The climax of the prayer for redemption is: "Sound the great shofar for our freedom; raise a banner to gather our exiles, and bring us together from the four corners of the earth into our land." The shofar shows us that true redemption and freedom only come when God provides us with victory, namely the Messiah (see Chapter 8 regarding the day of the blasting of the shofar). The word "freedom" appears in this sentence to remind us that the purpose of redemption is to free us from sin, that we serve God according to His will. The redemption won't come in a natural way, but through supernatural miracles: "Raise a banner to gather our exiles." The word "banner" here, נס, actually usually means a miracle, and this is a hint to a miraculous victory in the end times, though the literal translation is perfectly fine. A banner is used to declare victory over enemies, and Yeshua will provide the people of Israel with a miraculous victory; a sign that will cause them to come "together from the four corners of the earth into our land."

✦ Those who want to be part of the Kingdom of God should choose to stay away from:

a) Sin

b) The Jewish People

c) The Land of Israel

d) The State of Israel

The Redemption of Israel—The Land and the People

The Land of Israel and the people of Israel play important roles in God's plan to establish His Kingdom. This won't happen until the Jewish people return to the Promised Land and receive the Messiah, Yeshua from Nazareth. These conditions appear in many places in the Holy Scriptures, and here are a few examples:

> Therefore behold, days are coming declares the LORD and they will no longer say, "As the LORD lives, Who brought up the Children of Israel from the land of Egypt." Rather, "As the LORD lives Who lifted up and Who brought the seed of the House of Israel from the land of the north and from all the countries where I scattered them there and they shall dwell upon their land." (Jeremiah 23:7–8)

These verses point to the return of the people of Israel to their land and we can find hints about the future redemption. For example, the story of the Exodus from Egypt is mentioned in verse 7: "Who brought up the people of Israel out of the land of Egypt," is a story about redemption and the fact that it is mentioned here hints about Israel's future redemption. Verses 5 and 6 strengthen this argument: "Behold, days are coming, declares the LORD, when I will raise up for David, a righteous Branch, and He shall reign as King and deal wisely, and He will execute justice and righteousness in the land. In His days Judah will be saved, and Israel will dwell securely. And this is the name by which He will be called: 'The LORD our righteousness.'" These verses speak about our Righteous Messiah, and the days of the Messiah.

It is important that we pay attention to the relevance of these prophecies to the reality we live in today. "Out of the north country and out of all the countries where he had driven them. Then they shall dwell in their own land." This did not happen in the past until the return of the Jewish people to the Promised Land after two thousand years of exile. Additionally, the term "north country" refers to Ashkenaz and the former Soviet Union, from where most of the Jews who came to found the State of Israel came, as well as the many other "countries where he had driven them."

We find another example in the book of the Prophet Isaiah who spoke about the Jewish people's return to their land:

> It will be In that day, the LORD will extend His hand yet a second time to acquire the remnant of His people which remains from Assyria, from Egypt, from Pathros, from Cush, from Elam, from Shinar, from Hamath, and from the islands of the sea. He will raise a banner for the nations and will assemble the outcasts of Israel, and the dispersed of Judah, He will gather from the four corners of the earth. (Isaiah 11:11–12)

Verse 11 reveals important and interesting points that connect the past, present, and future. This verse starts with "In that day," which, according to the sages, were meant to show the reader that this period is prior to the establishment of the Kingdom of God. According to our sages, the phrase "in that day" refers to the Day of the Lord, the period when God will avenge and judge the nations that rose up against Israel. This verse continues: "The LORD will extend His hand yet a second time to recover the remnant that remains of his people." What does "extend His hand yet a second time" mean? As we have seen, the Prophet Jeremiah spoke about the first redemption of Israel coming out of the Land of Egypt. Here, Isaiah shows us that the day will come when God will save the remnant of His people—not only to take them out of exile, but for them to accept Messiah Yeshua and truly repent. This connects us to the situation today, where some of the people of Israel have already accepted the sacrifice of our Messiah Yeshua, though the majority still have not. The countries mentioned here are truly being gathered to Israel! "From Assyria (Kurdistan), from Egypt, from Pathros (upper Egypt), from Cush (Ethiopia), from Elam (Persia), from

Shinar (Iraq), from Hamath (Syria)". As we are being gathered, Messiah's coming is near.

Verse 12 starts with "He will raise a banner for the nations," which brings us back to God's promise to our forefathers that through the redemption of Israel, blessing and salvation will come upon all the nations, "And in you all the families of the earth shall be blessed." We find another example in Ezekiel's prophecy:

> And speak to them, thus said the LORD God, "Behold, I am taking the Children of Israel from among the nations which they went there. I will gather them from around, I will bring them to their land. I will make them for one nation in the land, in the mountains of Israel, and One King will be for them all for a king and there will no longer be two nations. They shall not be divided any longer into two kingdoms again. And they shall not be impure any longer in their idols and in their abominations and in all their transgressions. I will save them from all their dwelling places which they sinned there and I will purify them and they shall be for Me a people and I will be for them God. And My Servant David is King over them and One Shepherd will be for all of them and in My judgments they will walk and My statutes they will keep and they will do them. And they will dwell upon the land which I gave to My servant Jacob which your forefathers dwelt in it and they shall dwell upon it, they and their sons, and the sons of their sons forever and David My Servant is Prince for them forever. And I will cut for them a covenant of peace an eternal covenant it will be with them. I will give them and I will multiply them and I will put My sanctuary in their midst forever. And My tabernacle will be over them and I will be to them God and they will be to Me a people. The Gentiles will know that I am the LORD when I sanctify Israel, when My sanctuary is in their midst forever." (Ezekiel 37:21–28)

These verses speak about the day in which God Himself will take the children of Israel from the countries (nations) where they are scattered to the same Land that God promised and gave to Abraham, Isaac, and Israel. It is important to note the words "their own land," since this makes a connection between the people and land of Israel which God gave to them as an inheritance. Verse 22 opens with "And I will make them one nation in the land, on the mountains of Israel" (Judea and Samaria).

The expression "one nation" describes the unity that will be between the tribes, unity that will come to the people of Israel through the same King that is mentioned in this verse.

Verse 23 says: "They shall not defile themselves anymore with their idols and their detestable things, or with any of their transgressions. But I will save them from all the backslidings in which they have sinned, and will cleanse them; and they shall be my people, and I will be their God." This verse shows that Israel will continue to worship false gods until the time when God Himself will cleanse them: "And (I) will cleanse them; and they shall be My people, and I will be their God." The only way to be cleansed and worthy before God is through redemption that comes from accepting the sacrifice of Messiah Yeshua. Only in this way can Israel reach the state where we will be for Him a people and He will be for us a God. It's not a coincidence that in the next verse Ezekiel speaks about the Messiah: "My servant David will be King over them, and they will all have one Shepherd." As we have seen throughout the book, the words "My servant David" refers to the Messiah Himself, since only through Messiah can Israel fulfill her purpose as God's people, truly walking in God's path: "They will walk in My judgments and be careful to obey My statutes."

Throughout Scripture, when God repeats something several times we can assume that it has importance. Verse 25 says: "They will dwell in the land that I gave to My servant Jacob, where your fathers lived. They and their children and their children's children will dwell there forever." This verse emphasizes again the inseparable connection between the physical return of the children of Israel to the Land of Israel, and the plan for a greater number of the world to experience redemption. We also find in this verse a new aspect of this plan. The verse ends "forever." This shows us that there will never be another exile for the children of Israel, and it will remain that way until God's Kingdom, "And David My Servant shall be their prince forever." It is clear once again that "David" refers to the Messiah. These promises will be manifested through the New Covenant which God would make with Judah and Israel. "I will make a covenant of peace with them. It shall be an everlasting covenant with them." This is the same new covenant that the Prophet Jeremiah spoke of (see Jeremiah 31:31–34) as we have learned, which is based on the Messiah's work, just as Abraham's covenant was based on the Messiah's work.

Ezekiel continues and says: **"And I will cut for them a covenant of peace an eternal covenant it will be with them. I will give them and I will multiply them and I will put My sanctuary in their midst forever. And My tabernacle will be over them and I will be to them God and they will be to Me a people. The Gentiles will know that I am the LORD when I sanctify Israel, when My sanctuary is in their midst forever."**

This verses reminds us of the book of Revelation: "And I heard a great voice from heaven, saying 'Behold the tabernacle of God (is) with man, and He will dwell with them, and they will be His people and He will be with them God." (Revelations 21:3). Here we also see that the only way we can reach the time that we see the manifestation of the promise: "I will be their God, and they shall be my people" is through the future redemption of Israel.

Ezekiel 37 ends with the verse: "The nations will know that I am the LORD Who sanctifies Israel, when My sanctuary is in their midst forevermore." Here we see again that the realization of God's promises to His people Israel are connected to the redemption of the nations.

In conclusion, we have seen a close connection between the physical return of the people of Israel to the Land of Israel, and the spiritual repentance of the people of Israel through the Messiah of Israel, Yeshua of Nazareth.

CHAPTER 9

1) When Jews live in all of the Promised Land, the nations will have:

   a) Blessing

   b) War

   c) A headache

   d) High taxes

2) Moshe Rabbeinu said that Israel would be exiled because:

   a) The Land doesn't really belong to them

   b) The Arabs are more worthy

   c) Moses did not say such a thing

   d) The people of Israel would leave the covenant with God

3) God's plan to establish His Kingdom in this world depends on two things:

   a) The Messiah and the church

   b) The Messiah and the Jewish people

   c) Faith and lovingkindness

   d) The Holy Scriptures and the Holy Spirit

4) The concept "righteous one" (*tzaddik*/צדיק) doesn't refer to a perfect person, but to someone who has a good relationship with God.

   a) True

   b) False

5) The borders of the Land of Israel will be:

   a) Just as they are today

   b) As they were before the Six Day War (1967)

   c) Smaller than today for a Palestinian State

   d) From the river of Egypt to the Euphrates river.

6) According to the Bible, can the people of Israel appropriately serve God while they are in exile?

    a) Yes

    b) No

7) What must come before God establishes His Kingdom?

    a) All of the blessings that God promised

    b) Nothing—God's Kingdom can happen at any moment

    c) The Day of Judgment and divine justice

    d) Both A and B

8) The people of Israel will do so many good deeds that they will merit redemption and return to their land because of their loyalty, with nothing to do with God's mercy.

    a) True

    b) False

9) One of the signs of the final redemption is that Jews would return from:

    a) The land of the north

    b) All lands

    c) Both A and B

    d) No correct answer

10) There is a relationship between the New Covenant and:

    a) Abraham's covenant

    b) Moses' Torah

    c) David's covenant

    d) All of the above

11) God's promise regarding the Promised Land for the Jewish people is canceled because most of Israel refused to receive Yeshua as Messiah.

    a) True

    b) False

ANSWERS

1) A

2) D

3) B

4) True

5) D

6) No

7) C

8) False

9) C

10) D

11) False

HEBREW NUMEROLOGY AND THE BIBLE

Numbers appear in the Scripture much more often than most people may think. It is important to realize that numbers can and frequently do convey information which can figure greatly in arriving at the proper interpretation of a given passage of Scripture. In the same way that every word and every aspect of a word can provide insight to the one who interprets the Bible, so too is it necessary for the Bible student to understand the meaning of numbers.

Numerology can be abused and used by those who are not followers of the True Living God; therefore, it is important to state that the meaning of numbers which will be provided in this article will be supported by biblical texts alone and not the same meanings which may be traditional among Judaism or Christianity. One should be cautioned not to apply the significance of numbers to the occurrence of such numbers outside the Scriptures. For example, a person's birthday will not have any connection to the biblical significance for that number. Only when a number appears in the biblical text should one seek to discover if the number has any relevance to the interpretation of that particular number.

There are several rules in numerology that we must keep in order to stay away from an inaccurate interpretation of the text:

c) The only source we use to find the number's meaning is the Bible.

d) We must not apply the meaning of numbers from another area. For example, not to connect between the meaning of numbers and day-to-day life, such as birthdays, address, area code, etc.

In this appendix, every numerical interpretation is based on God's Word alone, though we are aware that there are different opinions in Judaism and Christianity regarding the meaning of numbers.

—— **Summary of Numerical Meaning, Which We Will Discuss Further** ——

One: God, unity

Two: Two divergent opinions, or differences

Three: Testing, revealing, proving, documenting, victory and if applied to God, holiness

Four: The world, four is the global number

Five: Incompletion or lacking

Six: Grace

Seven: Holiness, sanctification, purpose, and being set apart for a purpose (whether good or evil)

Eight: The Kingdom of God, redemption, and newness or renewal

Nine: Work, deed, outcome, result

Ten: Completion, wholeness, in a general sense, entirety

Twelve: People, the people of God

Thirteen: Unity between man and God, good things happen

Fourteen: A double blessing or God's providence

Seventeen: An emphasis on the meaning of the number seven, i.e. thoroughly sanctified, or completely or entirely set apart for a purpose

Eighteen: Life (according to Jewish tradition)

Thirty: Death

Forty: Transition or change

Fifty: Freedom and liberty

1
One

———————————————— **God, Unity** ————————————————

One refers to the LORD, Who is One. This number can also refer to unity. The first place the number "one" occurs is in Genesis 1:5. There one reads, "And there was an evening and there was a morning—one day." Later on in this same book of Genesis, it is stated concerning the man and his wife, "And they became one flesh" (Genesis 2:24). It is very significant that in both of these examples there was a multiplicity for the subject. In the first example, the evening and the morning became one day and in the second example, it was Adam and Eve who became one flesh.

One of the most famous passages in the Torah concerning God is Deuteronomy 6:4 which states, **"Hear O Israel the LORD your God the LORD is One."** The question which a person must ask himself is what is the connection between the use of the Hebrew word אחד, "one," which identifies a multiplicity being one and the fact that the LORD God of Israel is One? The answer is that the Hebrew word אחד can relate to the concept for one as in "unification". There is another Hebrew word that could have been used if the author wanted to refer to an absolute oneness or a singleness. This is the Hebrew word יחיד. In fact, there is a well-known prayer in Judaism which states, "אחד ואין יחיד כיחודו". This phrase should be translated as, "(God is) One and there is no singularity as His singularity." The idea that is being expressed in this prayer is that the LORD God of Israel is One; but not an absolute One; rather there is a uniqueness and a complexity to His Oneness.

The number one is frequently employed to express in the Scriptures one object, such as one man or one tabernacle. This usage would be the simple or common purpose that the number one or for that matter any number, would appear in a biblical text. Often the appearance of a number does not contain any of the significance that Hebrew numerology might offer. Therefore, the reader must always consider when coming across a verse which contains a number, that the number only expresses an amount and no additional significance.

Because the number one is often associated with God, there is a unique phenomenon in the Scriptures concerning this number. Sometimes the number one is employed to express a unique relationship that the object has to the LORD. For example, **"And it will be one day, it will be known to HaShem"** (Zechariah 14:7). In the text above, Zechariah could have stated simply, **"And it will be a day."** The fact that the prophet said **"one day"** is to convey that this day is uniquely related to God. Similarly, it is stated by the Prophet Ezekiel in chapter 37 **"one King"**, **"one nation"** and **"one Shepherd"** (see Ezekiel 37:22, 24). Each of these objects—King, nation, and Shepherd—have a connection to God. The King and Shepherd is Messiah Yeshua, the Son of God, and the one nation is Israel, the people of God.

2
Two

The classic example for the number "two" is found in Matthew chapter 26. There Yeshua says to His disciples, **"You know that after two days comes the Passover, and the Son of Man will be given over for crucifixion."** Matthew 26:2.

The phrase "after two days" is somewhat meaningless because after two days can mean three or more days. The period is unspecified. The reason for such ambiguous language is because the purpose of the number two in this passage is not solely numerical. This means that the text is not intending to provide the reader with some definite information concerning a time period. Rather, the purpose of the number two in this context is one of the numerological meanings of the number two. Often the number two relates to two divergent opinions. In the aforementioned verse, the author wants to inform the reader that there are two very different understandings for this coming Passover. Yeshua wants to emphasize that He is going up to Jerusalem in order to die as the true Passover sacrifice. Even though Yeshua states this emphatically, the disciples did not receive this. In fact, the disciples did not perceive at all what was going to take place during Passover in regard to Yeshua. In other words, Yeshua and the disciples have two divergent opinions concerning the Passover.

This same principle is also found in the Hebrew Bible. In the book of Amos one reads, **"Can two walk together without them having agreed"** (Amos 3:3). The word which was translated into English with the phrase "them having agreed" is נועדו. The root of this word is יעד which relates to a specific destination. The word which precedes this word is בלתי and in this context the word implies a change to the condition. In other words, had there not been a change in the condition, then the two could not walk together, i.e. they could not have arrived at the common destination.

The concept of divergent or different is also seen in the book of Genesis. In speaking about the sun and moon one reads, "And God made two great lights" (Genesis 1:16). Obviously the sun and moon are very different, as one is a source of light, while the latter just reflects light. Also in the book of Genesis, one encounters the account of the flood. Here Noah is commanded to bring onto the ark two sorts of each type of animal. In this passage, the two relates to two different (or divergent) kinds of the same sort, i.e., male and female. Likewise two angels came to Sodom, demonstrating that the people of Sodom had a very different way of living from that of the Law of God. Once again, the reader should not assume that every occurrence of the number two in the Bible demands this interpretation. However, one will find in a great majority of biblical passages, the reader will be assisted in arriving at the proper interpretation, when he considers this divergent quality for the number two.

3
Three

The number "three" is one of the most significant numbers in the Scriptures. Its primary purpose is for the sake of revealing or documenting something as fact (**testing** in order to validate something). It is also connected to the outcome of the will of God. One of the most famous occurrences for the number three is found in the book of Jonah, where Jonah is in the belly of the fish **"three days and three nights."** A major aspect of the book of Jonah is that the prophet was fleeing from the presence of the LORD. Instead of Jonah going to Nineveh as God had commanded, the prophet desired not to obey this commandment, even if it meant that his relationship with God would be destroyed.

The LORD decided to **test** in order to see if Jonah really preferred to end his relationship with God rather than go to Nineveh. By placing Jonah in the belly of the fish for three days and three nights, it would be revealed whether or not it was true that Jonah wanted to end his relationship with God over this commandment to go to Nineveh. It is most significant that immediately after (in the next verse) the reader is informed that Jonah was in the belly of the fish for three days and three nights. What does Jonah do? The text states that Jonah prayed to the LORD his God from within the fish. Hence, the three days and three nights ultimately revealed, proved, or documented that what Jonah said he wanted was not true. One could also say that Jonah was tested for those three days and three nights and the test results showed that he did not want to end his relationship with God and in the end Jonah went to Nineveh.

In a similar manner, Peter rejects Yeshua's statement that he will deny Him. Therefore Yeshua says to Peter that he will deny Him three times. These three denials prove, document, and reveal to the reader that Yeshua's statement was factual. It is not a coincidence that when Yeshua reinstated Peter after the resurrection, He asked him three times, **"Do you love Me?"** In this context, Yeshua was **testing** the validity of Peter's statement.

Yeshua also revealed that He, in a similar manner to Jonah being in the belly of the fish three days and three nights, would be in the belly of the earth three days and three nights and then rise from the dead. In this passage, the number three not only documents the fact that He died, but also the resurrection. It is also very significant that Yeshua rose on the third day.

The number three also relates to victory, as in the completion of God's purposes and plans. In the book of Genesis, one reads about the offering of Isaac. This passage has great theological significance and is one of the first passages which is read in the morning synagogue service each day. This section begins with the LORD commanding Abraham to offer his son as a burnt offering on one of the mountains in the land of Moriah. The climax of this portion of Scripture comes about on the third day. It was on the third day that HaShem provided the ram so that Isaac would live. In this passage, Isaac represents the promise (of God) which would have died (ended) had not the LORD acted. There is not a conflict between the two concepts for the number three of victory (the fulfillment of God's will) and revelation or documentation. Often, it is the climax of what HaShem is wanting to do which is simply being revealed or proved with the use of the number three.

Please note that when the number three is applied to God, then it can relate to holiness; whereas the number seven relates to holiness when this number is in reference to man (see explanation for the number seven).

4
Four

The number "four" has a global significance or relates to the world. There are some common and similar expressions in the Scripture which are **"the four winds of the heavens"** or **"the four corners of the earth"** or **"the four ends of the heavens."** Each of these expressions relate to the earth or the world in a collective manner. In the book of Daniel chapter 2, one reads about a dream which Nebuchadnezzar dreamed. In this dream, he saw an image set up and this image had four distinct parts. Each of these parts represented an empire which ruled over the world.

In the book of Deuteronomy chapter 22, Israel is told to make a four cornered garment and place a *tzitzit* upon each corner. The *tzitzit* represents the biblical commandments of the Torah (see Numbers chapter 15). These commandments are understood as being a framework for life in this world, as when one dies, the *tzitzit* are removed from one's four cornered garment for burial.

In the books of Ezekiel and Revelation, one encounters the four beasts which are in the heavens and never cease to praise HaShem. It is understood that the four beasts, who continuously say, **"Holy, Holy, Holy is the LORD God of Hosts, Who was and is and is to come"** (see Revelation 4:6–9) are related to the will of God for all the world (His creation). In a similar manner, one of the Seraphim called to another saying, **"Holy, Holy, Holy, is the LORD of Hosts, all of the earth (shall be) with His Glory."**

5
Five

In order for a person to understand the meaning of the number "five," one must first realize that the meaning of the number ten is completion or wholeness. Since five is half of ten, the idea is that the number five represents incompletion or that which is lacking. A Scripture that expresses this idea is found in the book of John. At a place called Beit Chesed (Bethesda), there was a pool whose waters healed the sick. The reader is told that around the pool there were five porches. It is stated that on these five porches lay individuals who were not whole. Some were paralyzed and the rest of them had a variety of health problems. It is not a chance happening that these people who were lacking their health were on five porches. Another well-known passage that contains the number five is found in I Samuel 17. In the account of David and Goliath, David picks up five stones (see I Samuel 17:40). Why is the reader told the specific number and not simply that David had gathered a few stones? The answer is to assist the reader in understanding that the stone which David hurled at Goliath was not the source of victory. Rather, this was only the means that God used to accomplish His victory. In other words, the stone and even David, who hurled this stone at Goliath, were insufficient to bring about this victory.

One of the first places where the idea of "lacking" or "incompleteness" is seen in regard to the number five is in the book of Genesis. In chapter 18, two angels are sent to Sodom to destroy the city. God tells Abraham that if fifty righteous people are found in the city, then the city will be free of this punishment (we will learn that the number fifty is related to freedom when this number is studied). This is revealed to Abraham and he responds saying, perhaps the city will lack fifty righteous people by five. It is significant that Abraham uses the number five when referring to the city lacking enough righteous people.

6
Six

The number "six" relates to the grace of God. It is not a coincidence that man was created on the sixth day of the week. The fact that man became a living being on the sixth day reveals that only by means of the grace of God will man experience true life, i.e., eternal life, through a relationship with God. In the book of Isaiah, there is a passage that is rich in theological truth. In chapter 6, one reads about the death of King Uzziah. It is this statement about Uzziah's death that sets the context for this passage. Next, the reader is given a vision of heaven with the LORD sitting on His throne. It is said about God that He is high and lifted up. The sages understand that the purpose of this phrase (high and lifted up) is to convey to the reader that there is a large separation between man and God. There is also mentioned in this vision of heaven that there were seraphim (a type of angel) present around the throne. It is revealed to the reader that each of the seraphim had six wings. The seraphim would call to one another saying, **"Holy, holy, holy, is the LORD of Hosts, full is the entire earth of His glory"** (Isaiah 6:3).

As a result of this proclamation concerning the holiness of God, the heavens shook and were filled with smoke. To this, the man Isaiah stated, **"Woe is me, for I am undone, for a man of unclean lips am I and in the midst of a people with unclean lips I dwell; for the King—the LORD of Hosts, my eyes have seen"** (Isaiah 6:5).

Isaiah is responding to the fact that he has just heard that the whole world is going to be full of the glory of God. It was this vision of a Holy God, Who was high and lifted up, that revealed to him his own sinfulness and the sinfulness of his people. His statement in verse five shows his hopelessness in and of himself. However, the next occurrence in this vision focuses upon the seraphim which had six wings. One of the seraphim flew to the altar and removed a burning ember and then touched the lips of Isaiah with it. Because of this act, the reader is informed that the iniquity of Isaiah is removed and his sin has been atoned. The point is that there is a direct connection to the six-winged seraph (seraphim in the plural) and the removal of iniquity and the atoning of sin. Theologically, one knows that the removal of iniquity and the atoning of sin are only the result of the grace of God.

Another reason that the number six is related to the grace of God is seen in the fact that there were six cities of refuge. A city of refuge was a type of safe haven for one who had killed an individual without direct intent of doing so. It was not seen as an accident; rather the Torah calls the killer a murderer. A family member of the one killed was commanded to slay the murderer; however the murderer could flee to one of the six cities of refuge and be safe within the walls of this city. In other words, although the murderer should die as the consequence of his action, he finds "grace" in the city of refuge. It is not a coincidence that there are six cities of refuge.

In the book of Ruth, the concept of redemption is a major theme. When Boaz agrees to act as the kinsman redeemer to Ruth, the reader is told that he gives her six measures of barley (Ruth 3:15). This again is not a chance happening. It is to reveal to the reader the relationship between grace (that which the number six expresses) and redemption. When speaking about the exodus from Egypt, which also came about through redemption (the Passover sacrifice), one finds that 600,000 men from the Hebrews came out of Egypt, i.e., experienced redemption (see Exodus 12:37). Once again the number six appears (600,000) to emphasize the connection between grace and redemption.

In the New Covenant there are several places where the number six appears and once again the context is grace. In Yochanan's (John) Gospel, the writer begins to speak about Passover. It has already been stated that Passover is known as the Festival of Redemption. In order to remind the reader of the connection between redemption and grace, Yochanan writes, **"Therefore Yeshua, six days before the Passover, came to Bethany"** (John 12:1).

Another interesting occurrence of the number six is also found in Yochanan's gospel. Here the context is also Passover. In this section, Yeshua speaks about the destruction of the Temple, which took forty and six years to build. He states that He will raise it up in three days (**here Yeshua is referring to His body**). How do these numbers assist the reader to arrive at a proper interpretation of the passage?

Although we have yet to study the significance of the number forty, we will learn that forty relates to a **transition** or **change**. John chapter 2 alludes clearly to the destruction of the Temple. Why will the Temple be destroyed? The answer is multifaceted. First, the message which the Temple service was suppose to convey to the people was so distorted by the corruption that characterized the Temple in Yeshua's day.

Second, the time was at hand for the grace of God to be revealed. It is important for the reader to remember that when Yeshua alluded to the Temple, He mentioned the forty and six years that it took for it to be built. Why was this fact necessary to be included in this passage? It is a hermeneutical aid to the reader. Forty and six speaks about a change or transition (the significance of the number forty) to grace (the meaning of the number six) and away from the sacrificial system of the Temple. The number three also appears in this discourse (see John 2:19). As we have already learned, the number three expresses a revealing or documentation. Hence, Yeshua was revealing (3) this change (40) from the sacrifices at the Temple, to the grace (6) of God, that His resurrection would document (3).

The final example which we will examine from the New Covenant is located in Matthew's gospel. In Matthew chapter 27, the context is once again Passover. In the passage in question, one reads, **"And from the sixth hour darkness was upon all the earth until the ninth hour"** (Matthew 27:45).

Matthew's gospel was written in a manner in which those from a Jewish background could easily grasp the significance of what he was stating. Jewish sages of old pointed out that because the exodus from Egypt took place in the night, there was a connection between darkness (the night) and redemption (the exodus from Egypt). In order to convey to Israel that this One Who hung upon the cross was in fact the Redeemer, HaShem caused a miracle to take place. As the verse states, there was darkness upon all the earth until the ninth hour. Although we have yet to study the significance of the number nine, let it suffice to say now that the number nine relates to "outcome" or "deed." Hence, the sixth hour is mentioned to relate to the grace of God and the ninth hour is recorded to reveal what was the outcome of the death of Yeshua, i.e., redemption.

7
Seven

Christianity frequently teaches that the meaning of the number seven is completion. This is not correct. The number seven relates to "rest" and "holiness." The best example of this is the many places where the number seven is used in regard to the Shabbat (the Sabbath day). The primary idea of the Shabbat is rest and holiness. Please note that there is also an etymological connection between the concept of holiness and sanctification. In several passages of Scripture, one reads that HaShem has sanctified the seventh day or He has made it holy. In addition to this, work is forbidden on the Shabbat. In fact, both biblically and traditionally, the Shabbat is seen as a day of rest.

Finally, the number seven can relate to perfection. Obviously there is an association between holiness and perfection.

What is the scriptural basis for those who teach that the number seven relates to completion? These scholars also refer to the Shabbat. In the book of Genesis, one reads, **"The heavens and the earth were finished (completed) and all their hosts. And God completed on the seventh day His work which He did and He ceased on the seventh day from all His work which He did"** (Genesis 2:1–2).

There certainly seems to be a biblical basis for associating the number seven with completion. However, in the next verse it is stated, **"And God blessed the seventh day and He sanctified it (literally made it Holy) for in it, He ceased (rested) from all His work which God created to do"** (Genesis 2:3).

Now we have two concepts related to seven, completion and holiness. When one examines the number seven in additional passages, the concept of holiness (sanctification) and perfection appear much more frequently. Before looking at a few such passages, let us refer to an additional verse that relates the number to completion. In Revelation 10:7, one reads that in the days of the seventh angel, the mystery of God should be finished (completed). The word that is translated "finished" or "completed" is the Greek word τελέω, which has great theological significance. There are two well known passages where this word appears. One is found in Romans chapter 10. Here the word in question is in the form of a noun. Although it is frequently translated as the "end," it is important for the reader to know that within this word there is the idea of "goal," "purpose," or "objective." The verse from Romans reads literally, **"For an end of Torah (is) Messiah for righteousness, for everyone who believes"** (Romans 10:4).

It is significant that there is no definite article (the) prior to the word "end." If the proper interpretation is that Yeshua brings an end to the Law, then the verse should state, "For **the** end of the Torah is Messiah." Most English translations insert the definite article, which the Greek text does not have. It is awkward to state, "an end." In actuality, Messiah did not bring an end to the Law; the Torah commandments continued to be practiced by the followers of Messiah (see Paul in Acts 21:20–24). The proper translation for this verse when understanding the fuller meaning of the word τέλος is, **"For an objective of the Law is Messiah; for righteousness for everyone who believes."**

The objective or purpose of the Law is not solely that people would turn to faith in Messiah. Naturally there are many purposes contained in the Torah. However, the Law reveals our unrighteousness and causes us to seek redemption by means of the Messiah. Although the Torah defines what is righteous (and unrighteous), it is only Yeshua Who can bring about righteousness in a person. Of course as the end of the verse states, Messiah only mediates righteousness for the one who believes.

The other passage that contains the word τελέω is John 19:30. In this verse, Yeshua is on the tree and knowing all things have been accomplished, He said, "It is finished." The emphasis of this statement is not that His work of redemption is complete, although this is true. Rather, this work was done in a perfect manner. Holiness is also related to purpose. It is very important for the Bible student to understand that holiness is always related to a purpose. As was briefly mentioned earlier, there is a strong relationship between the terms holiness and sanctification. In fact, both in Greek and in Hebrew the word sanctification is derived from the word holy. Hence, when Yeshua cried out, "It is finished," He is referring to the work that God the Father had set Him apart (sanctified Him) to do.

When considering another verse that has the number seven, the matter becomes clearer. Yeshua fed a multitude of 4,000 people from the seven loaves and few fishes. This is of course different from the feeding of the five thousand. After the multitude had eaten and were satisfied, the reader is told that seven full baskets were taken up. What is the meaning of the number seven in this passage? First, the number 4,000 (the number four, a thousand times) relates to the world. In examining the passage, perhaps a case could be made for asserting that Yeshua had come for the whole (complete) world. However, when taking into account the context of this section, another interpretation seems to fit better. Yeshua, in the previous paragraph, had healed the lame, deaf, blind, and the maimed. The emphasis is not simply that He had made them whole, but these are said to have glorified the God of Israel. In other words, these who were incapable of worshiping God, were now able to do so. The point is that Yeshua did not come to simply minister to the entire (complete) world, but to make the world holy, that is to sanctify the world according to His purposes. Likewise, when in the book of Revelation the seven spirits are mentioned (or the seven menorahs), the idea is not completion, but holiness and sanctification.

When the number ten is studied, it will be demonstrated that the concept of completion is much better applied to this number, rather than seven.

8
Eight

The number eight both in Judaism and Christianity expresses "newness." Many scholars call it the number of redemption or the Kingdom number. A common use for the number eight relates to circumcision, for a male child was circumcised on the eighth day. It was on the eighth day the male child was also given a name.

It was through the covenant of circumcision and the giving of a Hebrew name that the child entered into a new relationship as a member of the children of Israel. Circumcision also relates to the death of the flesh (carnal nature), which is one of the primary outcomes of redemption. Not living according to the flesh expresses a Kingdom lifestyle.

Before examining a few examples from the Scripture, let it be stated that early churches were often built with eight walls to convey faith in the resurrection (the Kingdom hope). The Bible states that Yeshua rose from the dead on the first day of the week. However, when also considering the prior week, seven days and adding the first day of the week, the total is eight. Therefore, Christianity has used the number eight to convey the concept of resurrection and not only the resurrection of Yeshua, but all who will enter into the Kingdom. Resurrection and Kingdom are often linked together in both Judaism and Christianity.

In the book of Leviticus, Moses provides a list of God's festival days. The last one is known as the Eighth Day Assembly (see Leviticus 23:36). Although very little is stated in the Scripture concerning this festival, it is treated as a Shabbat and called a holy convocation. Whereas Christianity ignores this day altogether, Judaism places great significance upon it and understands its message as related to the Kingdom.

A classic example of the number eight is found in Acts chapter 9. There, a man paralyzed for eight years, was healed by Peter. There is no coincidence that in the next passage the message found is resurrection. In 1 Peter 3:20, eight individuals are mentioned. These are Noah and his wife and their three sons and their wives. It was with these eight people that HaShem began humanity anew. This is one of the places where one can see how the concept of newness is related to the number eight. The vast majority of times the number eight appears in the Scripture it is part of a composite number. For example, in John chapter 5 a man was paralyzed for thirty and eight years (38). This occurrence provides a good illustration of how composite numbers should be handled.

Although the number thirty has as a general meaning of death, it is possible to understand it as multiplications of five and six, and three and ten. The idea then would be that when incompleteness (5) meets with the grace of God (6), there is a new beginning (8). One could make this interpretation somewhat more spiritual. As sinners we are incomplete (5) for entrance into the Kingdom of God, but when we experience the grace of God (6), we become a new creation (8) and are no longer incomplete for entrance into the Kingdom.

If one uses the other numbers (3 and 10) the following can be derived from the number 38. As we have learned, the number three expresses the concept of testing. Hence, the number thirty can relate to being thoroughly or completely (10) tested (3). Usually when a person finds himself being tested, he immediately prays for the testing to be stopped or to be removed from the trial. What is being expressed in this example is that one is going to be thoroughly or completely (10) tested (3) and when the purpose for this testing or trial is complete, then this person will have a new beginning (8).

9
Nine

The number nine is understood in Judaism to express the concepts of work, deed, outcome or result. A common illustration that is offered is a woman is pregnant for nine months and then the outcome/result of this pregnancy is manifested. Although the number appears several times in the Hebrew Scriptures, in general it is used to simply express an allotment of time; that is, something that happened in the ninth year. It is when one considers the appearance of the number nine in the New Covenant that the interpretation for the number becomes clear. In the book of Luke, Yeshua ministers to ten lepers. As these ten lepers obey Yeshua's command to go and show themselves to the priests, they were healed. Only one of those who were healed went back to thank Yeshua. The nine apparently continued on toward the priests. The point is that the one leper who returned to Yeshua really was the only one who was changed; the nine were only healed outwardly.

Biblically, leprosy is not the disease that most of the world usually assumes, a natural skin ailment that is highly contagious. In the Bible, leprosy is also highly contagious, but its cause is pride and unkind speech. Hence, it was the one who returned to Yeshua that really had been healed not only outwardly, but inwardly too, as he did not think of only being pronounced clean by the priests, but first he wanted to thank

Yeshua. Thanksgiving is an act of humility and not pride. The nine who were healed and did not return to Yeshua focused only on the outcome of the miracle. In other words, they only looked to the deed or the work of Yeshua and not the spiritual aspects of their situation.

When studying the number six, we also spoke about the number nine. Please note that many English translations, even some of the more literal ones, still make interpretations for the reader that are not warranted. This is often the case when hours (time of day) are mentioned. The ninth hour is actually three in the afternoon. Therefore, instead of leaving the text in its original manner, many translations prefer to change the ninth hour to three in the afternoon without informing the reader of the literal rendering. In doing so, the translation robs the reader of being able to benefit from the significance that a proper understanding of numbers adds to the text.

In the example given in our study of the number six, it is stated that there was darkness over the earth from approximately the sixth hour until the ninth (see Matthew 27:45). It was interpreted that the use of the numbers six and nine together expressed that Yeshua being on the cross was the deed/work (9) that made the grace of God (6) possible. Likewise, in the next verse (Matthew 27:46), Yeshua cries out at about the ninth hour, "My God, My God, why have You forsaken Me?" This statement speaks about the outcome/result of sin. Not Yeshua's sin (God forbid), as He was without sin! However, Scripture states that this One Who knew no sin; that God made Him sin for us, so we could become the righteousness of God in Him (2 Corinthians 5:21). The point is that Scripture mentions the ninth hour to reveal the outcome of Yeshua becoming sin on our behalf, i.e., His death. Sin and death are inherently related in the Bible, so it is also at the ninth hour the outcome/consequence of sin, is manifested. It is clear that Yeshua dying at the ninth hour was not a random happening. It pointed to the work of the Messiah, dying for the sins of the world.

10
Ten

The number ten relates to completion, wholeness, or speaking about something in its entirety. In Luke's gospel, Yeshua uses the number ten frequently in His parables or when recounting an event. Yeshua spoke of ten coins (chapter 15), ten lepers (chapter 17), ten servants (chapter 19), and ten units of money (chapter 19). In Matthew's Gospel, Yeshua refers to ten virgins; while in Mark's gospel, ten cities. In all these passages, Yeshua is utilizing the number ten in a collective manner. In other words, He is speaking about ten in a general manner or as a whole.

In the book of Revelation chapters 13 and 17, the number ten appears in reference to ten horns. These ten horns are related to the beast, which had also seven heads. These ten horns are ten kings who rule with the beast. Why specifically ten kings? Other than Israel, all the nations of the world are going to serve the beast. Hence, the ten kings represent the world in its entirety or wholeness. In this example, it may be puzzling at first to see why the number seven is used in regard to the beast, as seven relates to holiness or perfection. The solution to this difficulty is found when one remembers that seven also relates to purpose or setting something apart. Hence, the beast is the empire that has as its purpose the exact opposite of the will of God, i.e., the beast has been set apart to stand in opposition to the purposes of God.

In Hebrew, the word which relates to a pagan temple prostitute is the word that could be translated as a "holy one." Certainly this one is not holy in our understanding of the word; however in Hebrew, the idea that is being expressed by the use of the Hebrew word for "holy" is that this woman has been set apart (sanctified) for a purpose. Obviously a very unholy purpose; yet in Hebrew the word "holy" does not always convey a good or godly purpose, just a purpose.

12
Twelve

Naturally, when the number twelve is mentioned, two thoughts enter into one's mind. The first thought is the twelve tribes of Israel and the second is the twelve disciples. Both groups represent the people of God. Hence, when the number twelve appears in the Scriptures, the reader ought to think of the people of God in some unique or specific manner.

13
Thirteen

The meaning of the number thirteen is found when the numbers one and twelve are combined. We have learned that twelve refers to the people of God and the number one relates to HaShem; therefore, the number thirteen speaks of a unity between

God and His people. The classic example of this is found in the book of Joshua: **"All the cities of the children of Aaron, the Priests, (were) thirteen and their fields"** (Joshua 21:19). The priests' general calling was to serve in order to bring about unity between the LORD and His people.

The number thirteen is also seen when the people are commanded to make a special offering to God. There is a clear reference to thirteen bulls which were to be offered (see Numbers 29:13–14). Obviously, when the people made a sacrificial offering which was to be a pleasing aroma to the LORD, it is for the purpose of unity. This unity is not simply for the sake of unity, but for a mighty outcome which is the result from such a unity between God and His people. What is this outcome? The answer is victory, or the fulfillment of the will of God. In the book of Genesis, one reads that Ishmael was circumcised at the age of thirteen years.

Circumcision expresses the death of the flesh. In other words, the death of the flesh is the outcome of faith, the basis for the Abrahamic covenant. The death of the flesh represents the fulfillment of the will of God and the purpose of the LORD entering into a covenantal relationship with man. Again, the fulfillment of God's will relates to victory.

This same idea is subtly seen in the account of the walls of Jericho. The children of Israel were to march around the walls of Jericho one time for six days and on the seventh day (Shabbat) they were commanded to do so seven times. Rabbinical scholars point out that in all, the children of Israel marched around the city of Jericho thirteen times. When they fulfilled the commandment of HaShem, they were united with God through obedience to His Word, then the walls supernaturally crumbled into dust. This miraculous event gave the children of Israel victory. Hence, the number thirteen relates to unity between God and His people, which brings about victory. In this example, the number thirteen was comprised of the numbers six and seven. This reveals another aspect for the number thirteen. We have seen that unity speaks about the unity between man and God. The numbers six and seven are related to this idea. The only way that there can be unity between man and a Holy God is when sinners are made holy (7) by the grace of God (6).

In the book of Esther the number thirteen appears the most—six occurrences in all. Each of these occurrences is in regard to the thirteenth day of the twelfth month. Originally, this date represented the plan of Haman to destroy the Jewish people. It is most significant that this date was chosen in the first month, the month of Nisan, which is the month of redemption, i.e., Passover, for the Jewish people and in the twelfth year of the king. The reader needs to remember that the number twelve relates to the people of God. Therefore, the message the reader should derive from the verse (Esther 3:7) is that although Haman intended this date to be for the destruction of the Jewish people, the LORD intended it to be for the redemption of His people. In the end, the thirteenth day became known as the Fast of Esther. One of the primary purposes of fasting is to rid oneself of those things that are a hindrance between the one fasting and God. Hence, fasting is for the purpose of unity between man and God.

14
Fourteen

The idea that is expressed by the number fourteen is a double blessing or an expression of God's providence to His people. The rabbis point out that Jacob worked fourteen years and the outcome of these fourteen years of labor were his two wives, Leah and Rachel. A wife is a helpmate (Genesis 2:18) and the Scripture instructs that he who has found a wife has found a good thing (Proverbs 18:22). Hence, the outcome of these fourteen years of labor was the children of Israel (who were called to bless the world).

Passover is on the fourteenth day of the Jewish month of Nisan. Here again, according to the rabbis (Talmud—*Rosh HaShanah* 11a), not only did the first redemption take place on the fourteenth day of Nisan, so too, will the final redemption. The point is that this date, the fourteenth day of Nisan, will serve as a double blessing or a second expression of providence to His people. The first blessing was the exodus from Egypt into the land of promise, i.e., Israel; and the second blessing will be the exodus from sin into the Kingdom by means of our Passover Lamb, Yeshua the Messiah.

In a similar fashion, King Solomon dedicated the Temple during the Festival of Tabernacles. This festival is seven days; however, because Solomon wanted to express what a great blessing this was, he in fact celebrated for an additional seven days, i.e., fourteen days in total.

In the New Testament, the number fourteen appears in the very first chapter of Matthew's gospel. The reader is told that in Messiah's genealogy, there are fourteen generations between Abraham and David and fourteen generations between David and the Babylonian exile, and fourteen generations from the Babylonian exile to Messiah. It is understood that the Messiah is the second redeemer (Moses being the first) and the establishment of the Kingdom, being the role of Messiah, is the second expression of God's promise to His people of which the Prophets frequently spoke. Careful attention reveals that there were actually only thirteen generations from the Babylonian exile to the birth of Messiah. The fact that the text states fourteen is not an error. It is a subtle reference to not the first coming of Messiah, but to the second, when the Kingdom will be established. In Judaism, the final generation is often referred to as the next generation, so as to emphasize an expectancy for the Kingdom.

17
Seventeen

The number seventeen relates to the significance of the numbers ten and seven. In other words, the number seventeen expresses complete (10) sanctification. The example that is offered by Judaism is Joseph. In Genesis chapter 37, the reader is informed that he is going to encounter the genealogy of Jacob, but only one descendant is mentioned, Joseph. The first thing that is stated about Joseph is that he was seventeen years old (Genesis 37:2). What the reader learns about Joseph is that he goes through a series of trials for several years, all of which prepare him for the purpose of becoming the leader of the world. In other words, Joseph was set apart for a period of sanctification so that he could be prepared for the purpose of God.

When examining the Scripture, one finds the number seventeen clearly relating to the will of God, which relates to divine purpose. Once again, this setting apart for a purpose relates to the biblical concept of holiness. The Scripture states that the rain began to fall on the seventeenth day of the month (Genesis 7:11), that the ark came to a rest on the seventeenth day of the month (Genesis 8:4), Jacob lived in the land of Egypt seventeen years (Genesis 47:28), and that Jeremiah bought a field that was related to the will of God for seventeen shekels (Jeremiah 32:9).

18
Eighteen

Jewish tradition associates the number eighteen with the concept of life. The primary reason for this is when Hebrew letters are used to convey numbers (each Hebrew letter has a numerical value) the two letters which are used to express the number eighteen spell life. In the New Covenant, the number eighteen is found only in Luke chapter 13. There it appears three times (Luke 13:4, 11, and 16). Initially, Yeshua spoke about eighteen people whom the Tower of Shiloach fell upon and killed. This occurrence of the number eighteen would seem to relate to the opposite of life, i.e., death. However, it is important for the reader to understand the emphasis of the first section of this chapter is repentance. Next, Yeshua states, "Unless one repents, he shall perish." The message that Yeshua is teaching is repentance leads to life. The second and third time the number eighteen is discussed concerns a woman who has been bound by her infirmity for eighteen years. It was on the Shabbat that Yeshua healed her. In healing her, Yeshua remarked that it was proper that this woman be healed on the Shabbat, seeing that she, too, is a daughter of Abraham and was bound for eighteen years.

There are significant terms which Yeshua used in this passage. Shabbat relates to the Kingdom. The woman is called a daughter of Abraham. This term expresses the inheritance of the promise that God had made to Abraham, i.e., blessing. And lastly, the number eighteen is again mentioned. The lesson that the reader should take from this section is that repentance is fundamental to the Kingdom, i.e., the ultimate outcome of the Abrahamic Covenant. This all speaks to an abundant life, which the number eighteen conveys.

When examining the more than two dozen occurrences for the number eighteen in the Hebrew Scriptures, there is no clear connection of this number to life.

30
Thirty

The number thirty is understood in Judaism as relating to death. One of the mourning periods is known as a "Shaloshim." This is actually the Hebrew word for thirty. The connection between the number thirty and death is seen by the fact that the children of Israel mourned Aaron for thirty days (see Numbers 20:29). Likewise, when Moses died, the people also mourned him for exactly thirty days (see Deuteronomy 34:8). Another reference to the number thirty relating to death is found in the fact that Joshua took 30,000 men with him to fight Ai the second time (see Joshua 8:3). This time Israel was successful and Ai was put to death. It is significant that the reader is told that 12,000 people died, all the people of Ai (see Joshua 8:25). Here the number twelve, as in 12,000, relates to the people, as we learned in our study of the number twelve, and the fact that they all died is reflected in the 30,000 (30) soldiers that Joshua took.

In the New Covenant, the reader is told that Judas betrayed Yeshua, delivering Him over to the Jewish leadership to be put to death for thirty pieces of silver (see Matthew 26:15). In the book of Luke, it is revealed that Yeshua was about the age of thirty when He began His ministry. What was the primary aspect of Yeshua's ministry? In other words, what did Yeshua enter into this world to do? The answer is to offer up His life for redemption. Death is the key ingredient in redemption. As one reads, without the shedding of blood (death) there is no redemption.

40
Forty

Often people will speak of the number forty as a generational number. There is no evidence for such an interpretation from the Scripture. The number 40 expresses a change or transition. The examples for such a view are seen throughout the Bible.

- It rained for forty days in the days of Noah (see Genesis 7:12). These rains brought about a transition, HaShem would begin the world again with the family of Noah.

- Moses was on Mount Sinai for forty days and forty nights (see Exodus 34:28). Although this was the second time Moses went up to the mountain, it was this time that the Law was actually given to the children of Israel and a transition was made to Israel being commanded to observe the Law.

- Yeshua was tested in the mountains of Judah for forty days and forty nights (see Matthew 4:2) and afterward He began His ministry. Hence, a transition was made from when Yeshua did not minister, to the time when He began to fulfill His Father's will in a formal way.

- After the resurrection, Yeshua appeared for forty days (Acts 1:3) and He ascended into the heavens. Yeshua's earthly ministry had finished and there was a transition to His disciples carrying on His work.

- In the account of Absalom, the reader is told that at the end of forty years (see 2 Samuel 15:7), Absalom requested permission to go to Hebron from his father. Although he said that he wanted to pay his vows, this was said so he could depart and begin his rebellion against David, his father. Why is forty years mentioned? To what does the forty years refer? Some commentaries say the forty years was from when Saul began the monarchy. Whether this is true or not is undetermined. However, what is for sure is that there was a transition in the leadership of Israel.

The number forty appears in verse 7 to assist the reader in identifying this change in leadership.

Numerous other examples could be provided, but these few sufficiently demonstrate the meaning and use of the number forty in the Scriptures.

50
Fifty

When a person hears the number fifty the first thing that should enter his mind is Jubilee, for every fifty years was the Jubilee Year. In the book of Leviticus the following is read, **"And you shall sanctify the fiftieth year and you shall call (that year) a year of freedom in the Land for all the ones who dwell in it, it shall be a Jubilee for you"** (Leviticus 25:10).

The key word in this verse is the Hebrew word, דרור, which means freedom. When one studies the nature of this word for freedom, he will understand the relationship between freedom and the will of God. In other words, the freedom that is provided by God is so that His will can be realized in one's life. In connection with this understanding is another occurrence of the number fifty.

The Torah speaks of three special festivals that every Jewish male, twenty years and older must go up to Jerusalem to observe. These festivals are Unleavened Bread, Weeks, and Tabernacles. The Feast of Weeks derives its name from the fact that the LORD commanded the children of Israel to count seven weeks and the next day would be the Holy Day. However, during this time, not only were the children of Israel commanded to count seven weeks, but also fifty days. Hence, an additional name for the Festival of Weeks is Pentecost, or the festival of fifty. Although Judaism traditionally associates this festival with the giving of the Ten Commandments, it is only in the New Covenant that this festival is clearly connected to the giving of the Holy Spirit. It is important for the reader to comprehend that only when one is indwelt by the Holy Spirit can he truly turn away from the bondage of sin and be set free to obey the will of God.

Another example from the Scripture is found in the Gospels. Here, Yeshua fed the 5,000 (100 X 50). He had the 5,000 people sit down in groups of fifty. Because of this, there is obviously an emphasis on the number fifty. One of the theological points that this passage teaches is that when one acts in faith, he is not bound by the things of this world. Rather, he is free, or liberated, to serve God.

SUMMARY

Numbers can and often do assist the reader in arriving at a more accurate interpretation of biblical texts. In the examples provided in this article, one learns how to utilize the numbers that appear in the Bible and the rules/methodology for interpreting such numbers. Again, one must remember two important facts:

1) The significance of each number should only be applied to the numbers that appear in the Scriptures and not the numbers that we encounter in everyday life;

2) The significance of each number may not be relevant for every appearance of that number in the Scriptures. Hence, one should be very cautious in applying the significance of numbers when interpreting the Bible.

CONCLUSION

At the beginning of this book we noted that most people in the world wonder what the true meaning of their lives is, and they ask questions about life in our world: Is there life after death? Why do bad things happen? Is there anything beyond the world that we live in?

The Old Testament describes the source of life in the world in general and specifically human life, and one of the principles revealed through it is that it is impossible to completely understand life without knowing the Creator of the universe and Giver of Life.

Our hope is that through reading this book you received a basic understanding that answers these questions. It is important to note that in this book we didn't relate to the subject of the End of Days since in the future we will publish a different book on this subject.

If you still have not received eternal forgiveness through Messiah Yeshua and you wish to start living an eternal life with the Creator, all that you must do is say in your words this simple prayer:

> Our Father and God
>
> The God of Abraham, Isaac, and Jacob,
>
> The Torah by herself cannot save me, but to show me the need for redemption. Until today I didn't know your great love for me and the truth—that you are Holy and I am a sinner and I have no way to be righteous before you.
>
> I come now before you as I am and receive in faith the sacrifice of Messiah Yeshua, who you testified about in the Torah and Prophets, that we have atonement and forgiveness of sins.
>
> I believe that His blood purifies and justifies me, and gives me a pure heart and new spirit.
>
> Thank you, oh LORD, for the gift of the Holy Spirit!

Help me to walk in Yeshua's footsteps and to be a loyal disciple so
that I bring good fruit in abundance.

Amen!

If you only said the above prayer or already received the atonement of Messiah Yeshua in your life, we want to encourage you to read the book again and start to apply
the many points contained in it. Moreover, we want to encourage you to start to read
and study the Holy Scriptures day and night and apply them in your life:

> And Yeshua came before, speaking to them, saying, "All authority
> has been given to Me in the heaven and upon earth; therefore
> go, and make disciples of all nations, baptizing them in the name
> of the Father, and of the Son, and of the Holy Spirit, teaching
> them to keep all which I have commanded you. And behold, I am
> with you all the days, unto the completion of the age. Amen."
> (Matthew 28:18–20)

Remember that the One who was given all authority in heaven and on earth called
you to be a *disciple* and to make *disciples*. In the first stage you must be immersed in
an *immersion* of repentance and learn and teach to apply the Word of God in your
life and in the lives of those around you.

Finally, always remember that when you are in Messiah Yeshua you are never alone
and the same One who was given authority in heaven and earth is with you every day
and every moment until the end of time. Amen.